JEOPARDY!

TM

What Is Quiz Book 2?

Other Books

Jeopardy! . . . What Is Quiz Book 1?

JEOPARDY!™

What Is Quiz Book 2?

**Andrews McMeel
Publishing**

Kansas City

Jeopardy! ... What Is Quiz Book 2?

Book design by Holly Camerlinck

ISBN: 0-7407-0573-3

Attention: Schools and Businesses

JEOPARDY!™

What Is Quiz Book 2?

JEOPARDY!

AMERICAN LITERATURE

"THE COLOR PURPLE" IS THE BEST-KNOWN WORK BY THIS GEORGIA-BORN WOMAN	**$100**	WHO IS
TO RESEARCH "AIRPORT", HE SPENT HOURS IN AIRPORTS ABSORBING THE ATMOSPHERE	**$200**	WHO IS
HEMINGWAY TOOK THE TITLE OF THIS NOVEL ABOUT JOURNALIST JAKE BARNES FROM A PASSAGE IN ECCLESIASTES	**$300**	WHAT IS
"NATURE", AN 1836 ESSAY BY THIS TRANSCENDENTALIST & FRIEND OF THOREAU, WAS PUBLISHED ANONYMOUSLY	**$400**	WHO IS
IN CHAPTER 2 OF "TOM SAWYER", TOM CONS OTHER BOYS INTO HELPING HIM WITH THIS TASK	**$500**	WHAT IS

JEOPARDY!

AMERICAN LITERATURE

$100	WHO IS ALICE WALKER?	**$100**
$200	WHO IS ARTHUR HAILEY?	**$200**
$300	WHAT IS "THE SUN ALSO RISES"?	**$300**
$400	WHO IS RALPH WALDO EMERSON?	**$400**
$500	WHAT IS WHITEWASHING A FENCE?	**$500**

JEOPARDY!™

BIBLICAL HOTTIES

DURING GOD'S FIRST CONVERSATION WITH MOSES, IT WAS ON FIRE BUT "WAS NOT CONSUMED"	**$100**	WHAT IS
ANGELS HAD TO DRAG LOT & HIS FAMILY OUT OF THIS CITY BEFORE THINGS GOT TOO HOT	**$200**	WHAT IS
IT WAS HEATED 7 TIMES HOTTER THAN NORMAL FOR SHADRACH, MESHACH & ABEDNEGO	**$300**	WHAT IS
THIS VEHICLE "OF FIRE" ON WHICH ELIJAH ASCENDED INTO HEAVEN WAS A REAL "HOT ROD"	**$400**	WHAT IS
ON THIS HOLY DAY, TONGUES OF FIRE APPEARED TO THE APOSTLES, WHO THEN BEGAN TO SPEAK IN TONGUES	**$500**	WHAT IS

JEOPARDY!

BIBLICAL HOTTIES

$100   WHAT IS THE BURNING BUSH? $100

$200   WHAT IS SODOM? $200

$300   WHAT IS THE (FIERY) FURNACE? $300

$400   WHAT IS THE CHARIOT (OF FIRE)? $400

$500   WHAT IS PENTECOST? $500

4

JEOPARDY!

JOHN HUGHES FILMS

Clue	Value	Response
IT'S THE 1990 STORY OF AN 8-YEAR-OLD BOY ACCIDENTALLY ABANDONED AT CHRISTMAS	**$100**	WHAT IS
TITLE CHARACTER WHO SAYS, "THIS IS MY NINTH SICK DAY THIS SEMESTER . . . SO I BETTER MAKE THIS ONE COUNT"	**$200**	WHO IS
MOLLY RINGWALD'S FAMILY FORGETS HER BIRTHDAY WHILE PREPARING FOR HER SISTER'S WEDDING IN THIS FILM	**$300**	WHAT IS
STEVE MARTIN & JOHN CANDY USE THESE TITLE MODES OF TRANSPORTATION TO TRY TO GET HOME FOR THANKSGIVING	**$400**	WHAT ARE
HE PLAYED THE BRAINY BRIAN IN "THE BREAKFAST CLUB"	**$500**	WHO IS

JEOPARDY!

JOHN HUGHES FILMS

$100	WHAT IS "HOME ALONE"?	**$100**
$200	WHO IS FERRIS BUELLER?	**$200**
$300	WHAT IS "SIXTEEN CANDLES"?	**$300**
$400	WHAT ARE "PLANES, TRAINS & AUTOMOBILES"?	**$400**
$500	WHO IS ANTHONY MICHAEL HALL?	**$500**

JEOPARDY!

COUGH, COUGH

Clue	Value	Response
COMMON NAME OF PERTUSSIS	$100	WHAT IS
THESE BROTHERS STARTED SELLING THEIR COUGH DROPS IN 1847	$200	WHO ARE
A SHORT, DRY COUGH, OR A TRITE WRITER FOR HIRE	$300	WHAT IS
THE MEN'S MALADY A DOCTOR IS USUALLY CHECKING FOR AFTER HE ASKS THE PATIENT TO "TURN YOUR HEAD AND COUGH"	$400	WHAT IS
THIS COUGH SUPPRESSANT IS AN OPIUM DERIVATIVE	$500	WHAT IS

JEOPARDY!

COUGH, COUGH

$100   WHAT IS WHOOPING COUGH? $100

$200   WHO ARE THE SMITH BROTHERS? $200

$300   WHAT IS A HACK? $300

$400   WHAT IS A HERNIA? $400

$500   WHAT IS CODEINE? $500

JEOPARDY!

LET'S CROSS THAT BRIDGE

BEFORE ITS COMPLETION IN 1917, THE QUEBEC RAILWAY BRIDGE OVER THIS RIVER COLLAPSED TWICE	$100	WHAT IS
CLEVELANDER HART CRANE'S POEM "THE BRIDGE" PRAISES THIS ONE ACROSS NYC's EAST RIVER	$200	WHAT IS
THIS TYPE OF MOVABLE BRIDGE THAT PRO-TECTED CASTLES IS ALSO USED TO PERMIT RIVER TRAFFIC	$300	WHAT IS
RIVER CROSSED BY THE ALLENBY, OR KING HUSSEIN, BRIDGE	$400	WHAT IS
PUENTE DE PIEDRAS IS A CENTURIES-OLD BRIDGE IN THIS COUNTRY WHERE "THE BRIDGE OF SAN LUIS REY" IS SET	$500	WHAT IS

JEOPARDY!

LET'S CROSS THAT BRIDGE

$100   WHAT IS THE ST. LAWRENCE RIVER? $100

$200   WHAT IS THE BROOKLYN BRIDGE? $200

$300   WHAT IS A DRAWBRIDGE? (ACCEPT: BASCULE) $300

$400   WHAT IS THE JORDAN? $400

$500   WHAT IS PERU? $500

JEOPARDY!

WHEN WE COME TO "_IT_"

A CATCHER'S CATCHER	**$100**	WHAT IS
"QUICK" ONES ARE FAST WITH A JOKE; "HALF" ONES DON'T GET THE JOKE	**$200**	WHAT ARE
ON TV, YOU CAN FIND "CAROLINE IN" IT	**$300**	WHAT IS
YOU WON'T FIND "CAROLINE IN" THIS MEDIUM-SIZED ITALIAN TUBULAR PASTA	**$400**	WHAT IS
SOMETHING MOVING IN IRREGULAR BURSTS GOES IN THESE "AND STARTS"	**$500**	WHAT ARE

JEOPARDY!

WHEN WE COME TO "_IT_"

$100   WHAT IS A MITT? $100

$200   WHAT ARE WITS? $200

$300   WHAT IS THE CITY? $300

$400   WHAT IS ZITI? $400

$500   WHAT ARE FITS? $500

DOUBLE JEOPARDY!

BUCHANAN . . . JAMES BUCHANAN

A GOOD FRIEND OF BUCHANAN'S WAS THIS MAN WHO WENT ON TO BE PRESIDENT—OF THE CONFEDERACY	**$200**	WHO IS
BUCHANAN WAS BORN IN THE TOWN OF STONY BATTER IN THIS STATE; HE DIED & WAS BURIED IN LANCASTER THERE	**$400**	WHAT IS
BUCHANAN WAS ON BOTH SIDES OF THE FENCE FOR THIS NUMERICAL BOUNDARY OF OREGON THAT POLK WANTED	**$600**	WHAT IS
IN THE 1856 ELECTION, BUCHANAN BEAT THIS FORMER PRESIDENT WHO RAN AS A KNOW-NOTHING	**$800**	WHO IS
BUCHANAN DIDN'T LIKE THIS ILLINOIS "LITTLE GIANT" THOUGH HE MAY HAVE GIVEN MONEY TO BUCHANAN'S CAMPAIGN	**$1000**	WHO IS

13

DOUBLE JEOPARDY!
BUCHANAN . . . JAMES BUCHANAN

$200 — WHO IS JEFFERSON DAVIS? — $200

$400 — WHAT IS PENNSYLVANIA? — $400

$600 — WHAT IS "FIFTY-FOUR FORTY"? — $600

$800 — WHO IS MILLARD FILLMORE? — $800

$1000 — WHO IS STEPHEN DOUGLAS? — $1000

DOUBLE JEOPARDY!

JAZZ NICKNAMES

Clue	Value	Response
HE WAS KNOWN AS POPS AS WELL AS SATCHMO	$200	WHO IS
WITH THIS NICKNAME, JULIAN EDWIN ADDERLY BARRELLED DOWN "THEM DIRTY BLUES"	$400	WHAT IS
ORAN PAGE, TRUMPETER & ACCOMPANIST TO BESSIE SMITH, WAS KNOWN AS THIS, LIKE A "M*A*S*H" CHARACTER	$600	WHAT IS
HE GAINED FAME AS THE "HI DE HO" MAN	$800	WHO IS
THAT HE WAS BORN AS AN ARMANDO IN 1941 SHOULD TELL YOU THIS "CHICK" IS A GUY	$1000	WHO IS

DOUBLE JEOPARDY!

JAZZ NICKNAMES

$200	WHO IS LOUIS ARMSTRONG? **$200**
$400	WHAT IS CANNONBALL? **$400**
$600	WHAT IS HOT LIPS? **$600**
$800	WHO IS CAB CALLOWAY? **$800**
$1000	WHO IS CHICK COREA? **$1000**

DOUBLE JEOPARDY!

BUSINESS FOUNDERS

IN THE 19th C. HE FLED THE GERMAN MILITARY DRAFT & WENT ON TO BREW BEER IN GOLDEN, COLORADO	**$200**	WHO IS
TODD McFARLANE'S CAREER DRAWING SPIDERMAN FOR THIS COMICS LINE SPAWNED HIS OWN PRIVATE COMPANY	**$400**	WHAT IS
IN 1968 ROBERT NOYCE & GORDON MOORE FOUNDED THIS MICRO-CHIP COMPANY & SOON BROUGHT ANDREW GROVE ON BOARD	**$600**	WHAT IS
THE COMPANY FOUNDED BY THIS MAN IN 1876 DEVELOPED INSULIN, MANY ANTIBIOTICS & PROZAC	**$800**	WHO IS
"UNCLE HERB" KELLEHER FOUNDED THIS NO-FRILLS AIRLINE NAMED FOR A QUADRANT OF THE U.S.	**$1000**	WHAT IS

DOUBLE JEOPARDY!

BUSINESS FOUNDERS

$200	WHO IS ADOLPH COORS?	**$200**
$400	WHAT IS MARVEL?	**$400**
$600	WHAT IS INTEL? (ACCEPT: INTEGRATED ELECTRONICS)	**$600**
$800	WHO IS (COLONEL) ELI LILLY?	**$800**
$1000	WHAT IS SOUTHWEST AIRLINES?	**$1000**

DOUBLE JEOPARDY!

THE COMICS

TESS TRUEHEART IS THE SWEETHEART OF THIS POLICE DETECTIVE DRAWN BY CHESTER GOULD	$200	WHO IS
ON JANUARY 1, 1995 "THE FAR SIDE" ENDED; ON DECEMBER 31, 1995 THIS BILL WATTERSON STRIP DID, TOO	$400	WHAT IS
BRENDA STARR'S LONGTIME JOB	$600	WHAT IS
IN THE STRIP "CROCK", QUENCH IS ONE OF THESE ANIMALS	$800	WHAT IS
"UNCLEAR ON THE CONCEPT" IS A COMMON THEME IN THIS JOE MARTIN STRIP	$1000	WHAT IS

DOUBLE JEOPARDY!

THE COMICS

$200	WHO IS DICK TRACY?	**$200**
$400	WHAT IS "CALVIN & HOBBES"?	**$400**
$600	WHAT IS REPORTER?	**$600**
$800	WHAT IS A CAMEL?	**$800**
$1000	WHAT IS "MR. BOFFO"?	**$1000**

DOUBLE JEOPARDY!

CHEM LAB

GLENN SEABORG, A DISCOVERER OF THIS DEADLY ELEMENT, SAID IT WAS GIVEN THE SYMBOL Pu "AS A JOKE"	**$200**	WHAT IS
GASOLINE IS MADE UP OF HUNDREDS OF THESE, THE SIMPLEST ORGANIC COMPOUNDS	**$400**	WHAT ARE
IT'S DEFINED AS THE CHEMISTRY OF SUBSTANCES THAT LACK CARBON BONDS	**$600**	WHAT IS
THIS COLORLESS GAS IS THE VC IN PVC	**$800**	WHAT IS
THE GREEK PREFIX MEANING "EQUAL" IS USED IN THIS TERM FOR 2 FORMS OF THE SAME ELEMENT	**$1000**	WHAT IS

DOUBLE JEOPARDY!

CHEM LAB

$200	WHAT IS PLUTONIUM?	$200
$400	WHAT ARE HYDROCARBONS?	$400
$600	WHAT IS INORGANIC CHEMISTRY?	$600
$800	WHAT IS VINYL CHLORIDE?	$800
$1000	WHAT IS ISOTOPE?	$1000

DOUBLE JEOPARDY!

GIMME AN "F"

A TYPE OF UNDER-THE-TABLE FLIRTING IS CALLED "PLAYING" THIS	$200	WHAT IS
SHARK PART THAT'S SLANG FOR A 5-DOLLAR BILL	$400	WHAT IS
THE U.S.S. CONSTITU-TION IS ONE OF THE MOST FAMOUS OF THESE SAILING SHIPS	$600	WHAT ARE
THOMAS GRAY WROTE, "WHERE IGNORANCE IS BLISS, 'TIS" THIS "TO BE WISE"	$800	WHAT IS
SOME CALL THIS ISLAND COUNTRY THE "CROSSROADS OF THE SOUTH PACIFIC"	$1000	WHAT IS

DOUBLE JEOPARDY!

GIMME AN "F"

$200 WHAT IS FOOTSIE(S)? **$200**

$400 WHAT IS A FIN? **$400**

$600 WHAT ARE FRIGATES? **$600**

$800 WHAT IS "FOLLY"? **$800**

$1000 WHAT IS FIJI? **$1000**

HAMLET

THE GRAVEDIGGER SAYS HAMLET WAS SENT TO THIS COUNTRY BECAUSE "THERE THE MEN ARE AS MAD AS HE"

WHAT IS

FINAL JEOPARDY!
HAMLET

WHAT IS ENGLAND?

JEOPARDY!

THE BIG APPLE

SHEEP MEADOW & THE TURTLE POND CAN BE FOUND IN THIS 843-ACRE PUBLIC PLAYGROUND	**$100**	WHAT IS
ONE WORLD TRADE CENTER IS THE TALLEST BUILDING IN THE CITY; THIS IS THE SECOND TALLEST	**$200**	WHAT IS
A MAST TO MOOR DIRIGIBLES WAS ADDED TO THIS SKYSCRAPER, BUT ONLY ONE EVER MOORED SUCCESSFULLY	**$300**	WHAT IS
HE WAS INAUGURATED FOR HIS SECOND TIME AS MAYOR OF NEW YORK CITY JANUARY 1, 1998	**$400**	WHO IS
THERE'S A STATUE OF THIS "YANKEE DOODLE DANDY" "OVER THERE" IN TIMES SQUARE	**$500**	WHO IS

JEOPARDY!™

THE BIG APPLE

$100	WHAT IS CENTRAL PARK?	**$100**
$200	WHAT IS TWO WORLD TRADE CENTER?	**$200**
$300	WHAT IS THE EMPIRE STATE BUILDING?	**$300**
$400	WHO IS RUDOLPH W. GIULIANI?	**$400**
$500	WHO IS GEORGE M. COHAN?	**$500**

JEOPARDY!

NONFICTION

THIS "DILBERT" CANINE'S "TOP SECRET MANAGEMENT HAND-BOOK" IS A HUMOROUS GUIDE FOR EXECUTIVES	**$100**	WHO IS
"A SIMPLE PATH" IS A COMPILATION OF THIS NOBEL PRIZE-WINNING NUN'S THOUGHTS & EXPERIENCES	**$200**	WHO IS
FOR THE WEEK OF OCTOBER 12, 1997, 3 OF THE TOP 4 N.Y. TIMES PAPERBACK BESTSELLERS WERE ABOUT HER	**$300**	WHO IS
IN "INTO THIN AIR" JON KRAKAUER SAID CLIMBING THIS MOUNTAIN "WAS PRIMARILY ABOUT ENDURING PAIN"	**$400**	WHAT IS
THIS SLUGGER PRAISED THE "ORIOLE WAY" OF TEACHING BASEBALL IN "THE ONLY WAY I KNOW"	**$500**	WHO IS

JEOPARDY!™

NONFICTION

$100 | WHO IS DOGBERT? | **$100**

$200 | WHO IS MOTHER TERESA? | **$200**

$300 | WHO IS PRINCESS DIANA? | **$300**

$400 | WHAT IS MOUNT EVEREST? | **$400**

$500 | WHO IS CAL RIPKEN, JR.? | **$500**

JEOPARDY!

SUPERSTITIONS

Clue	Value	Response
THIS APPENDAGE MAY BE CONSIDERED LUCKY, BUT NOT FOR THE ORYCTOLAGUS CUNICULUS	**$100**	WHAT IS
"FIND" ONE OF THESE & "PICK IT UP, ALL DAY LONG YOU'LL HAVE GOOD LUCK"	**$200**	WHAT IS
ST. PATRICK MIGHT HAVE TOLD A DIFFERENT STORY IF HE'D BEEN "LOOKING OVER" THIS LUCKY PLANT	**$300**	WHAT IS
TOSSING THIS AT NEWLYWEDS IS SUPPOSED TO ENSURE THE COUPLE'S FERTILITY	**$400**	WHAT IS
THIS MAN FOUNDED A RELIGION, SO GO AHEAD & RUB HIS TUMMY FOR LUCK	**$500**	WHO IS

JEOPARDY!

SUPERSTITIONS

$100	WHAT IS A RABBIT'S FOOT?	**$100**
$200	WHAT IS A PENNY? (ACCEPT: PIN)	**$200**
$300	WHAT IS A FOUR-LEAF CLOVER?	**$300**
$400	WHAT IS RICE?	**$400**
$500	WHO IS BUDDHA?	**$500**

JEOPARDY!

SPORTS

Clue	Value	Response
THIS CHICAGO BULL SET A PLAYOFF RECORD WITH A 63-POINT GAME ON APRIL 20, 1986	$100	WHO IS
THIS NFL QUARTERBACK IS A GREAT-GREAT-GREAT-GRANDSON OF BRIGHAM YOUNG	$200	WHO IS
THE NABISCO DINAH SHORE IS ONE OF THE 4 EVENTS MAKING UP THE GRAND SLAM OF THIS SPORT FOR WOMEN	$300	WHAT IS
THIS OAKLAND A's & NEW YORK YANKEES OUTFIELDER HIT .357 WITH 10 HOME RUNS IN HIS 5 WORLD SERIES	$400	WHO IS
LAST NAME OF BROTHERS PHIL & TONY, BOTH NAMED TO THE HOCKEY HALL OF FAME	$500	WHAT IS

JEOPARDY!™

SPORTS

$100	WHO IS MICHAEL JORDAN?	**$100**
$200	WHO IS STEVE YOUNG?	**$200**
$300	WHAT IS GOLF?	**$300**
$400	WHO IS REGGIE JACKSON?	**$400**
$500	WHAT IS ESPOSITO?	**$500**

JEOPARDY!

NOT-SO-MAD SCIENTISTS

THE "E" IN HIS MOST FAMOUS EQUATION STANDS FOR ENERGY, NOT HIS NAME	$100	WHO IS
THIS MONK CONCEIVED THE LAWS OF HEREDITY WHILE MINDING HIS PEAS & Qs AS A TEACHER IN BRUNN, AUSTRIA	$200	WHO IS
JAMES WATSON & FRANCIS CRICK TEAMED UP TO DISCOVER THE DOUBLE HELIX STRUCTURE OF THIS	$300	WHAT IS
HIS DISCOVERIES PUBLISHED IN THE 1704 WORK "OPTICKS" EXPLAINED WHY OBJECTS APPEAR TO BE COLORED	$400	WHO IS
IN 1920 THIS DANE BECAME DIRECTOR OF THE INSTITUTE FOR THEORETICAL PHYSICS IN COPENHAGEN	$500	WHO IS

JEOPARDY!

NOT-SO-MAD SCIENTISTS

$100	WHO IS ALBERT EINSTEIN?	$100
$200	WHO IS (GREGOR JOHANN) MENDEL?	$200
$300	WHAT IS DNA? (ACCEPT: DEOXY-RIBONUCLEIC ACID)	$300
$400	WHO IS SIR ISAAC NEWTON?	$400
$500	WHO IS NIELS BOHR?	$500

JEOPARDY!

"C.C."

AT THIS FLORIDA SITE, THE SCIENTISTS ARE ALL OUT TO LAUNCH	$100	WHAT IS
HIS NAME, PRE-MUHAMMAD ALI	$200	WHO IS
COMPUTER DATABASES HAVE LARGELY REPLACED THIS LIBRARY RESOURCE	$300	WHAT IS
SLICES OF SALAMI, BOLOGNA, LIVERWURST, ETC.	$400	WHAT ARE
IN 1968 THIS LABOR LEADER HAD A GRAPE, ER...GRIPE	$500	WHO IS

JEOPARDY!

"C.C."

$100   WHAT IS CAPE CANAVERAL? $100

$200   WHO IS CASSIUS CLAY? $200

$300   WHAT IS A CARD CATALOG? $300

$400   WHAT ARE COLD CUTS? $400

$500   WHO IS CESAR CHAVEZ? $500

DOUBLE JEOPARDY!

1910

KENT STATE & BOWLING GREEN STATE UNIVERSITIES OPENED IN THIS STATE IN 1910	**$200**	WHAT IS
THIS TRADE PAPER OF THE GARMENT INDUSTRY BEGAN PUBLISHING JULY 13, 1910	**$400**	WHAT IS
THE DESIGN OF THIS NYC RAILROAD STATION THAT OPENED IN 1910 WAS BASED ON THE ROMAN BATHS OF CARACALLA	**$600**	WHAT IS
THE AUTHOR OF "THE BATTLE HYMN OF THE REPUBLIC", SHE WENT MARCHING ON TO THE GREAT BEYOND OCT. 17, 1910	**$800**	WHO IS
IN 1910 E.M. FORSTER PUT A FINISH TO THIS NOVEL ABOUT A COUNTRY HOUSE	**$1000**	WHAT IS

39

DOUBLE JEOPARDY!

1910

$200	WHAT IS OHIO?
$400	WHAT IS WOMEN'S WEAR DAILY? (ACCEPT: WWD)
$600	WHAT IS PENN(SYLVANIA) STATION?
$800	WHO IS JULIA WARD HOWE?
$1000	WHAT IS "HOWARDS END"?

DOUBLE JEOPARDY!

LIBATIONS

Clue	Value	Response
IT'S THE MOST FAMOUS COCKTAIL WE KNOW WITH SINGAPORE IN ITS NAME	**$200**	WHAT IS
BE IT THE WHISKEY OR ANOTHER TYPE, THIS COCKTAIL SHOULD BE MADE WITH FRESH LEMON JUICE	**$400**	WHAT IS
WHISKEY & VERMOUTH ARE THE MAIN INGREDIENTS IN THE CLASSY COCKTAIL NAMED FOR THIS ISLAND	**$600**	WHAT IS
ON "M*A*S*H" TRAPPER JOHN ONCE ASKED A BARTENDER TO KEEP POURING THIS "HORRI-FYING" DRINK "UNTIL I TURN INTO ONE"	**$800**	WHAT IS
THIS YELLOW, ANISE-FLAVORED LIQUEUR IS AN ESSENTIAL INGREDIENT IN A HARVEY WALLBANGER	**$1000**	WHAT IS

DOUBLE JEOPARDY!

LIBATIONS

$200	WHAT IS A SINGAPORE SLING?	**$200**
$400	WHAT IS A SOUR?	**$400**
$600	WHAT IS MANHATTAN?	**$600**
$800	WHAT IS A ZOMBIE?	**$800**
$1000	WHAT IS GALLIANO?	**$1000**

DOUBLE JEOPARDY!

TIM CONWAY FILMS

TIM APPEARED WITH SANDRA BULLOCK IN THE 1997 SEQUEL TO THIS FILM, BUT HE DIDN'T REPLACE KEANU REEVES	**$200**	WHAT IS
IN 2 1960s MOVIES BASED ON THIS SERIES, TIM REPRISED HIS TV ROLE OF ENSIGN PARKER	**$400**	WHAT IS
TIM TEAMED UP WITH THIS FELLOW TV COMEDIAN IN SEVERAL FILMS INCLUDING 1980's "THE PRIVATE EYES"	**$600**	WHO IS
TIM HELPS A SHAPE-SHIFTING DEAN JONES RUN FOR OFFICE IN THIS SEQUEL TO "THE SHAGGY DOG"	**$800**	WHAT IS
IN A 1975 FILM, TIM PLAYED AMOS, A BUMBLING BANK ROBBER, WHO JOINS THIS TITLE GANG NAMED FOR A DESSERT	**$1000**	WHAT IS

DOUBLE JEOPARDY!

TIM CONWAY FILMS

$200	WHAT IS "SPEED"?	**$200**
$400	WHAT IS "McHALE'S NAVY"?	**$400**
$600	WHO IS DON KNOTTS?	**$600**
$800	WHAT IS "THE SHAGGY D.A."?	**$800**
$1000	WHAT IS "THE APPLE DUMPLING GANG"?	**$1000**

DOUBLE JEOPARDY!

COMMON BONDS

SPY, LOOKING, STAINED	**$200**	WHAT ARE
BACHELOR'S, PANIC, BELLY	**$400**	WHAT ARE
UNSTIRRED MARTINIS, A LEG, YOUR BOOTY	**$600**	WHAT ARE
SHOULDER, ROLLER, SLING	**$800**	WHAT ARE
RIVER, SNOW, BLOOD	**$1000**	WHAT ARE

DOUBLE JEOPARDY!

COMMON BONDS

$200   WHAT ARE TYPES OF GLASS? $200

$400   WHAT ARE BUTTONS? $400

$600   WHAT ARE THINGS YOU SHAKE? $600

$800   WHAT ARE BLADES? $800

$1000   WHAT ARE BANKS? $1000

DOUBLE JEOPARDY!

AT EASEL

PICASSO'S "GUERNICA" WAS INSPIRED BY THE BOMBING OF A TOWN IN THIS, HIS NATIVE COUNTRY	**$200**	WHAT IS
THIS DUTCHMAN WHO DIED IN 1669 GAVE US PERHAPS THE MOST PENETRATING SELF-PORTRAITS IN ALL OF ART	**$400**	WHO IS
HEH-HEH, HEH-HEH, THIS CARTOONIST WHO CREATED "BEAVIS AND BUTT-HEAD" WAS INFLUENCED BY MONTY PYTHON	**$600**	WHO IS
THE FIRST NAME OF PROTO-BAROQUE PAINTER CARAVAGGIO, & OF RENAISSANCE PAINTER-SCULPTOR BUONAROTTI	**$800**	WHAT IS
BORN IN 1869, HE EXCELLED AS A POINTILLIST, A FAUVIST & FINALLY, AS A COLLAGIST	**$1000**	WHO IS

DOUBLE JEOPARDY!

AT EASEL

$200   WHAT IS SPAIN? $200

$400   WHO IS REMBRANDT (VAN RIJN)? $400

$600   WHO IS MIKE JUDGE? $600

$800   WHAT IS MICHELANGELO? $800

$1000   WHO IS HENRI MATISSE? $1000

DOUBLE JEOPARDY!

OH, POOH!

Clue	Value	Response
HE WAS AUTHOR A.A. MILNE'S SON IN REAL LIFE, POOH'S OWNER IN FICTION	$200	WHO IS
THIS SWEET IS POOH'S FAVORITE FOOD	$400	WHAT IS
THIS DONKEY FRIEND OF POOH LATER PUT OUT A "GLOOMY LITTLE INSTRUCTION BOOK"	$600	WHO IS
ERNEST H. SHEPARD CONTRIBUTED TO THE ORIGINAL POOH BOOKS IN THIS CAPACITY	$800	WHAT IS
IT'S THE "SIZABLE" FOREST WHERE WINNIE-THE-POOH & HIS FRIENDS LIVE	$1000	WHAT IS

DOUBLE JEOPARDY!

OH, POOH!

$200 | WHO IS CHRISTOPHER ROBIN (MILNE)? | $200

$400 | WHAT IS HONEY? | $400

$600 | WHO IS EEYORE? | $600

$800 | WHAT IS THE ILLUSTRATOR? | $800

$1000 | WHAT IS THE HUNDRED ACRE WOOD? | $1000

FINAL JEOPARDY!
FAMOUS STRUCTURES

IN 1930 THE CHRYSLER
BUILDING SURPASSED THIS
FOREIGN STRUCTURE BY
OVER 60 FEET TO BECOME
THE WORLD'S TALLEST

WHAT IS

FINAL JEOPARDY!
FAMOUS STRUCTURES

WHAT IS THE EIFFEL TOWER?

JEOPARDY!

YOU GO, GIRL!

IT WAS THE MAIN CLAIM TO FAME OF A 26-YEAR-OLD RUSSIAN WOMAN NAMED VALENTINA TERESHKOVA	$100	WHAT IS
KNOWN AS "FLO JO", AT THE 1988 OLYMPICS SHE COULD GO LIKE NO OTHER GIRL	$200	WHO IS
JEANA, A PILOT ON THE FIRST NONSTOP, NON-REFUELING AROUND-THE-WORLD FLIGHT, SHARES THIS LAST NAME WITH SUPERPILOT CHUCK	$300	WHAT IS
SHE SET ALL KINDS OF SPEED RECORDS BEFORE DISAPPEARING IN JULY 1937	$400	WHO IS
IN THIS WORK, ONE OF THE BIG TALKERS ON THEIR WAY TO BECKET'S TOMB IS A PRIORESS, MADAME EGLENTYN	$500	WHAT IS

JEOPARDY!™

YOU GO, GIRL!

$100	WHAT IS THE FIRST WOMAN IN SPACE?	**$100**
$200	WHO IS FLORENCE GRIFFITH JOYNER?	**$200**
$300	WHAT IS YEAGER?	**$300**
$400	WHO IS AMELIA EARHART?	**$400**
$500	WHAT IS "THE CANTERBURY TALES"?	**$500**

JEOPARDY!

MUSIC POTPOURRI

Clue	Value	Response
"ANATOMICAL" TERM FOR THE PART OF A STRING INSTRUMENT WHERE YOU'LL FIND THE FINGERBOARD	$100	WHAT IS
SOME PIANOS HAVE A THIRD, "SUSTAINING" ONE OF THESE	$200	WHAT IS
ON SHEET MUSIC, ff STANDS FOR THIS ITALIAN WORD THAT MEANS "VERY LOUD"	$300	WHAT IS
THIS FAMOUS SINGING GROUP BASED IN AUSTRIA'S CAPITAL WAS FOUNDED OVER 500 YEARS AGO, IN 1498	$400	WHAT IS
BEETHOVEN CALLED IT "SONATA QUASI UNA FANTASIA", BUT WE KNOW IT BY THIS "LUNAR" NAME	$500	WHAT IS

JEOPARDY!

MUSIC POTPOURRI

$100   WHAT IS THE NECK? $100

$200   WHAT IS A PEDAL? $200

$300   WHAT IS FORTISSIMO? $300

$400   WHAT IS THE VIENNA BOYS' CHOIR? $400

$500   WHAT IS "MOONLIGHT SONATA"? $500

JEOPARDY!

SCIENTIFIC NAMES

LITTLE RED RIDING HOOD COULD TELL YOU IT'S KNOWN AS CANIS LUPUS	**$100**	WHAT IS
THE DOMESTIC TYPE OF THIS ANIMAL IS EQUUS CABALLUS	**$200**	WHAT IS
PANTHERA LEO, IT'S SEEN BEFORE MGM FILMS	**$300**	WHAT IS
THIS WHITE CREATURE IS URSUS MARITIMUS	**$400**	WHAT IS
WE SUPPOSE THIS BIRD, MEGADYPTES ANTIPODES, IS NAMED PARTLY FOR ITS NATIVE REGION	**$500**	WHAT IS

JEOPARDY!

SCIENTIFIC NAMES

$100	WHAT IS THE (GRAY OR TIMBER) WOLF?	**$100**
$200	WHAT IS THE HORSE?	**$200**
$300	WHAT IS THE LION?	**$300**
$400	WHAT IS THE POLAR BEAR?	**$400**
$500	WHAT IS THE PENGUIN?	**$500**

JEOPARDY!

BOND WOMEN

THE COLOR SHIRLEY EATON WAS PAINTED ALL OVER HER BODY	**$100**	WHAT IS
AS JAMES BOND'S OLD FLAME, TERI HATCHER WAS PUT OUT IN THIS 1997 FILM	**$200**	WHAT IS
THIS SWISS BOMBSHELL SET THE STYLE FOR GIRLS TO COME WITH HER BODY OF WORK AS HONEY RYDER IN "DR. NO"	**$300**	WHO IS
THIS "LICENSE TO KILL" CO-STAR LATER GOT A LICENSE TO PRACTICE "LAW AND ORDER"	**$400**	WHO IS
NATALIE'S SISTER, SHE WAS PLENTY O'TOOLE IN "DIAMONDS ARE FOREVER"	**$500**	WHO IS

JEOPARDY!™

BOND WOMEN

$100	WHAT IS GOLD?	**$100**
$200	WHAT IS "TOMORROW NEVER DIES"?	**$200**
$300	WHO IS URSULA ANDRESS?	**$300**
$400	WHO IS CAREY LOWELL?	**$400**
$500	WHO IS LANA WOOD?	**$500**

JEOPARDY!

U.S. GEOGRAPHY

IT'S THE ONLY STATE LYING SOUTH OF THE TROPIC OF CANCER	**$100**	WHAT IS
THIS 36-MILE-LONG RIVER PROVIDES PART OF THE BORDER BETWEEN NEW YORK & ONTARIO	**$200**	WHAT IS
THIS HISTORIC GEORGIA PORT LIES ON A RIVER OF THE SAME NAME, 18 MILES INLAND FROM THE ATLANTIC	**$300**	WHAT IS
THIS ARTIFICIAL LAKE IS NEVADA'S ONLY LAKE WITH AN OUTLET TO THE SEA	**$400**	WHAT IS
RHODE ISLAND'S SAKONNET & SEEKONK RIVERS ARE REALLY SALTWATER ARMS OF THIS BAY	**$500**	WHAT IS

JEOPARDY!

U.S. GEOGRAPHY

$100   WHAT IS HAWAII?   **$100**

$200   WHAT IS THE
NIAGARA RIVER?   **$200**

$300   WHAT IS SAVANNAH?   **$300**

$400   WHAT IS LAKE MEAD?   **$400**

$500   WHAT IS
NARRAGANSETT BAY?   **$500**

JEOPARDY!

BEFORE & AFTER

THE ONETIME FLYING NUN WHO LANDS ON A MAGICAL BASEBALL DIAMOND ON YOUR FARM	$100	WHO IS
VAMPIRE LESTAT CREATOR WHO'S A "SAN FRANCISCO TREAT"	$200	WHO IS
DISAFFECTED GROUP BORN AFTER 1965 WHO ARE INVESTIGATED BY MULDER & SCULLY	$300	WHAT IS
THE LEAD SINGER OF THE MIRACLES WHO WAS STRANDED ON A DESERT ISLAND	$400	WHO IS
A BASKIN-ROBBINS TREAT USED FOR TOP SECRET DISCUSSION ON "GET SMART"	$500	WHAT IS

JEOPARDY!™

BEFORE & AFTER

$100   WHO IS SALLY FIELD OF DREAMS? $100

$200   WHO IS ANNE RICE-A-RONI? $200

$300   WHAT IS GENERATION X-FILES? (ACCEPT: GEN X-FILES) $300

$400   WHO IS SMOKEY ROBINSON CRUSOE? $400

$500   WHAT IS THE ICE CREAM CONE OF SILENCE? $500

64

DOUBLE JEOPARDY!

GOOD WILL SHAKESPEARE

WILL SHAKESPEARE'S FATHER JOHN WAS A BUSINESSMAN IN THIS TOWN & ONCE HELD AN OFFICE EQUAL TO MAYOR	**$200**	WHAT IS
WILL'S CHILDREN HAMNET & JUDITH WERE THESE, LIKE DROMIO & DROMIO IN "THE COMEDY OF ERRORS"	**$400**	WHAT ARE
WILL'S BIRTH IS CELEBRATED ON APRIL 23 PARTLY BECAUSE THAT'S THE FEAST DAY OF THIS PATRON SAINT OF ENGLAND	**$600**	WHO IS
IN LONDON SHAKESPEARE BOARDED WITH THE MOUNTJOYS, A FAMILY OF THESE FRENCH PROTESTANTS	**$800**	WHAT ARE
A PERPLEXING BEQUEST IN WILL'S WILL LEFT WIFE ANNE THE SECOND-BEST ONE OF THESE	**$1000**	WHAT IS

DOUBLE JEOPARDY!

GOOD WILL SHAKESPEARE

$200 — WHAT IS STRATFORD (UPON AVON)? — $200

$400 — WHAT ARE TWINS? — $400

$600 — WHO IS ST. GEORGE? — $600

$800 — WHAT ARE HUGUENOTS? — $800

$1000 — WHAT IS A BED? — $1000

DOUBLE JEOPARDY!

NAMES IN THE NUDE

ON A MEMORABLE AWARDS SHOW, JIM CARREY MODELED THIS BIBLICAL ACCESSORY & SAID, "THIS IS WHERE FASHION BEGAN"	**$200**	WHAT IS
THIS MODEL LOOKED M'M! M'M! GOOD IN THE DECEMBER 1999 ISSUE OF PLAYBOY	**$400**	WHO IS
IN 1997 BRAD PITT SUED THIS MAGAZINE FOR PUBLISHING NUDE PHOTOS OF HIM	**$600**	WHAT IS
ROBERT CARLYLE & MARK ADDY WERE 2 STARS OF THIS BRITISH FILM ABOUT HAPLESS MALE STRIPPERS	**$800**	WHAT IS
DEMI MOORE SHED HER CLOTHES & HER HAIR TO PLAY A NAVY SEAL IN THIS 1997 FILM	**$1000**	WHAT IS

DOUBLE JEOPARDY!

NAMES IN THE NUDE

$200	WHAT IS A FIG LEAF?	$200
$400	WHO IS NAOMI CAMPBELL?	$400
$600	WHAT IS PLAYGIRL?	$600
$800	WHAT IS "THE FULL MONTY"?	$800
$1000	WHAT IS "G.I. JANE"?	$1000

DOUBLE JEOPARDY!

19th CENTURY AMERICA

IN 1849 STAGECOACH MAIL DELIVERY SERVICE WAS INTRODUCED ON THIS TRAIL BETWEEN MISSOURI & NEW MEXICO	**$200**	WHAT IS
THESE 2 MEN FOUGHT A FATAL DUEL ON JULY 11, 1804 IN WEEHAWKEN, NEW JERSEY	**$400**	WHO ARE
ON DEC. 15, 1893 DVORAK'S 9th SYMPHONY, KNOWN AS THIS, WAS PREMIERED BY THE N.Y. PHILHARMONIC	**$600**	WHAT IS
ON MAR. 29, 1882 THIS FIRST FRATERNAL SOCIETY OF CATHOLIC MEN WAS FOUNDED IN NEW HAVEN, CONNECTICUT	**$800**	WHAT IS
THIS 1803 CASE WAS THE FIRST IN WHICH THE SUPREME COURT DECLARED AN ACT OF CONGRESS UNCONSTITUTIONAL	**$1000**	WHAT IS

DOUBLE JEOPARDY!

19th CENTURY AMERICA

$200	WHAT IS THE SANTA FE TRAIL?	**$200**
$400	WHO ARE AARON BURR & ALEXANDER HAMILTON?	**$400**
$600	WHAT IS THE "NEW WORLD" SYMPHONY?	**$600**
$800	WHAT IS THE KNIGHTS OF COLUMBUS?	**$800**
$1000	WHAT IS MARBURY VS. MADISON?	**$1000**

DOUBLE JEOPARDY!

ICE CREAM

Clue	Value	Response
IN 1988 A 4 1/2-MILE ONE OF THESE FRUITY DESSERTS WAS CREATED IN PENNSYLVANIA	**$200**	WHAT IS
MINTY PYTHON & CHOC NESS MONSTER WERE SUGGESTIONS FOR THIS DUO'S NEW BRITISH FLAVOR	**$400**	WHO ARE
MID-20th CENTURY ELECTRIC REFRIGERATORS MEANT NO MORE WAITING FOR FROZEN TREATS UNTIL HE COMETH	**$600**	WHAT IS
THIS CHAIN ONCE BOASTED OVER 1,000 RESTAURANTS SERVING 28 FLAVORS WITH 16% BUTTERFAT	**$800**	WHAT IS
IN THE 1980s RESTAURATEUR DAVID MINTZ BEGAN MARKETING SOY ICE CREAM UNDER THIS BRAND NAME	**$1000**	WHAT IS

DOUBLE JEOPARDY!

ICE CREAM

$200	WHAT IS A BANANA SPLIT?	**$200**
$400	WHO ARE BEN & JERRY?	**$400**
$600	WHAT IS THE ICEMAN?	**$600**
$800	WHAT IS HOWARD JOHNSON'S?	**$800**
$1000	WHAT IS TOFUTTI?	**$1000**

DOUBLE JEOPARDY!

NOTORIOUS

A BOOK ON THIS NIXON VICE PRESIDENT'S FORCED RESIGNATION WAS TITLED "A HEARTBEAT AWAY"	**$200**	WHO IS
AFTER KILLING THIS CRIMINAL FOR THE $10,000 REWARD, BOB FORD MADE PERSONAL APPEARANCES & WAS BOOED	**$400**	WHO IS
HE WAS HANGED, DRAWN & QUARTERED IN FRONT OF PARLIAMENT JAN. 31, 1606; NOT A GOOD "DAY" FOR HIM	**$600**	WHO IS
AN ASSASSIN'S AX ENDED THE LIFE OF THIS RUSSIAN REVOLUTIONARY IN MEXICO IN 1940	**$800**	WHO IS
THIS MAFIOSO TURNED SONGBIRD IN THE '60s WITH HIS TESTIMONY & HIS 1968 "PAPERS"	**$1000**	WHO IS

DOUBLE JEOPARDY!

NOTORIOUS

$200   WHO IS SPIRO AGNEW? $200

$400   WHO IS JESSE JAMES? $400

$600   WHO IS GUY FAWKES? $600

$800   WHO IS LEON TROTSKY? $800

$1000   WHO IS JOSEPH VALACHI? $1000

DOUBLE JEOPARDY!

ANT-ONYMS

MOST MEMBERS OF AN ANT COLONY ARE THESE, AS OPPOSED TO RESTERS	**$200**	WHAT ARE
LIKE TERMITES, ANTS ARE THIS TYPE OF INSECT, NOT SOLITARY	**$400**	WHAT IS
IF YOU WANT A MOUND BUILT TO DAMAGE FARM MACHINERY, HIRE THESE ANTS WHOSE NAME IS AN ANTONYM OF "HIRE"	**$600**	WHAT ARE
AMAZON ANTS BECOME MASTERS WHEN THEY STEAL THE YOUNG FROM OTHER NESTS & MAKE THEM THESE	**$800**	WHAT ARE
THE EXTINCT PASSENGER PIGEON & THIS AFRICAN ARMY ANT ARE BOTH KNOWN FOR MOVING IN HUGE SWARMS	**$1000**	WHAT IS

DOUBLE JEOPARDY!

ANT-ONYMS

$200   WHAT ARE WORKERS? $200

$400   WHAT IS SOCIAL? $400

$600   WHAT ARE FIRE ANTS? $600

$800   WHAT ARE SLAVES? $800

$1000   WHAT IS THE DRIVER ANT? $1000

FINAL JEOPARDY!

ISLANDS

THIS ISLE IS ROUGHLY AT THE CENTER OF THE TRIANGLE FORMED BY DUBLIN, GLASGOW & LIVERPOOL

WHAT IS

FINAL JEOPARDY!

ISLANDS

WHAT IS THE ISLE OF MAN?

JEOPARDY!™

PENNSYLVANIA

Clue	Value	Response
IT WAS AT THIS COLD HISTORIC SITE THAT VON STEUBEN REORGANIZED OUR ARMY IN FEBRUARY 1778	$100	WHAT IS
ONE OF ITS MORE UNIMAGINATIVE NICKNAMES IS "THE CAPITAL OF THE KEYSTONE STATE"	$200	WHAT IS
PITTSBURGH'S CIVIC ARENA WAS THE FIRST PUBLIC AUDITORIUM TO HAVE A RETRACTABLE ONE OF THESE	$300	WHAT IS
PHILADELPHIA'S MAJOR LEAGUE TEAMS INCLUDE THE PHILLIES, EAGLES, 76ers & THIS HOCKEY TEAM	$400	WHAT ARE
THIS PORT CITY DISPLAYS A RECONSTRUCTION OF OLIVER HAZARD PERRY'S SHIP, THE NIAGARA	$500	WHAT IS

JEOPARDY!

PENNSYLVANIA

$100	WHAT IS VALLEY FORGE?	**$100**
$200	WHAT IS HARRISBURG?	**$200**
$300	WHAT IS A ROOF?	**$300**
$400	WHAT ARE THE FLYERS?	**$400**
$500	WHAT IS ERIE?	**$500**

80

JEOPARDY!

ALMOST RHYMES WITH ORANGE

Clue	Value	Response
TO ADAPT EXISTING MUSIC FOR A PERFORMER, AS NELSON RIDDLE DID FOR FRANK SINATRA	$100	WHAT IS
A CEREAL COOKED IN WATER OR MILK & EATEN FOR BREAKFAST; BABY BEAR'S WAS "JUST RIGHT"	$200	WHAT IS
THIS ADJECTIVE MEANING "ALIEN" MIGHT RHYME WITH ORANGE IF YOU REVERSED THE FINAL "GN" & ADDED AN E	$300	WHAT IS
A TUBE FITTED WITH A PLUNGER & NEEDLE, USED TO INJECT FLUIDS	$400	WHAT IS
THE ITALIAN CITY OF THIS NAME HAS IL DUOMO; THE ONE IN SOUTH CAROLINA HAS THE PEE DEE EXPERIMENT STATION	$500	WHAT IS

JEOPARDY!

ALMOST RHYMES WITH ORANGE

$100 WHAT IS ARRANGE? **$100**

$200 WHAT IS PORRIDGE? **$200**

$300 WHAT IS FOREIGN? **$300**

$400 WHAT IS A SYRINGE? **$400**

$500 WHAT IS FLORENCE? **$500**

JEOPARDY!

PRISON PROSE

Clue	Value	Response
IN "CIVIL DISOBEDI-ENCE", HE CALLED HIS NIGHT IN CONCORD JAIL "NOVEL AND INTERESTING ENOUGH"	$100	WHO IS
TITLE OF SISTER HELEN PREJEAN'S BOOK ABOUT DEATH ROW & THE SUSAN SARANDON FILM BASED ON IT	$200	WHAT IS
A WORK BY JEAN GENET STEMS FROM TIME AT THIS TYPE OF "SCHOOL", NAMED FOR WHAT IT TRIES TO DO TO YOUTHS	$300	WHAT IS
IN 1981 JAILED WRITER JACK HENRY ABBOTT WAS SPRUNG WITH THE HELP OF THIS "EXECUTIONER'S SONG" AUTHOR	$400	WHO IS
HITLER'S CHIEF ARCHITECT, HE WROTE "SPANDAU: THE SECRET DIARIES" OF HIS TIME IN PRISON FOR WAR CRIMES	$500	WHO IS

JEOPARDY!

PRISON PROSE

$100	WHO IS HENRY DAVID THOREAU?	**$100**
$200	WHAT IS "DEAD MAN WALKING"?	**$200**
$300	WHAT IS (METTRAY) REFORM SCHOOL? (ACCEPT: REFORMATORY)	**$300**
$400	WHO IS NORMAN MAILER?	**$400**
$500	WHO IS ALBERT SPEER?	**$500**

JEOPARDY!

TO THE NEAREST . . .

TO THE NEAREST 100, NUMBER OF YEARS THE UNITED STATES OF AMERICA HAS BEEN AN INDEPENDENT NATION	**$100**	WHAT IS
TO THE NEAREST FOOT, THE HEIGHT OF PATRICK EWING, ALONZO MOURNING OR RIK SMITS	**$200**	WHAT IS
TO THE NEAREST 10, THE BOILING POINT OF WATER IN FAHRENHEIT DEGREES	**$300**	WHAT IS
TO THE NEAREST BILLION, NUMBER OF COKES YOU'D NEED TO BUY TO GIVE ONE TO EVERYONE IN THE WORLD	**$400**	WHAT IS
TO THE NEAREST HOUR, FLIGHT TIME OF THE CONCORDE FROM LONDON TO NEW YORK	**$500**	WHAT IS

JEOPARDY!

TO THE NEAREST . . .

$100	WHAT IS 200?	**$100**
$200	WHAT IS 7?	**$200**
$300	WHAT IS 210?	**$300**
$400	WHAT IS 6 (BILLION)?	**$400**
$500	WHAT IS 4?	**$500**

JEOPARDY!

SUPERMAN

Clue		Response
THIS CUB REPORTER WAS CREATED FOR THE RADIO SERIES & LATER ADDED TO THE COMIC BOOK	**$100**	WHO IS
THE FAMOUS COVER OF ACTION COMICS NO. 1 SHOWS SUPERMAN LIFTING ONE OF THESE	**$200**	WHAT IS
RUMOR SAYS HE WAS SET TO DO ANOTHER SEASON OF "SUPERMAN" WHEN HE DIED IN 1959	**$300**	WHO IS
IN THE 1978 "SUPERMAN" MOVIE, GENE HACKMAN PLAYED THIS VILLAIN	**$400**	WHO IS
SUPERMAN HAS 2 SETS OF PARENTS: JONATHAN & MARTHA IN KANSAS, & LARA & THIS FATHER ON KRYPTON	**$500**	WHO IS

JEOPARDY!

SUPERMAN

$100 WHO IS JIMMY OLSEN? **$100**

$200 WHAT IS A CAR? (ACCEPT: SEDAN) **$200**

$300 WHO IS GEORGE REEVES? **$300**

$400 WHO IS LEX LUTHOR? **$400**

$500 WHO IS JOR-EL? **$500**

JEOPARDY!

3-LETTER SCIENCE

Clue	Value	Response
YOU'RE "WISER" IF YOU KNOW IT'S A SMALL POINTED STRUCTURE ON A STEM THAT GROWS INTO A FLOWER OR A LEAF	$100	WHAT IS
ABOUT 4.5 BILLION YEARS OLD, IT'S THE CLOSEST G2 TYPE STAR TO WHERE YOU'RE STANDING	$200	WHAT IS
YOU ADD THIS ELEMENT TO COPPER & ZINC TO GET BRONZE	$300	WHAT IS
A NEUTRAL ATOM WILL BECOME ONE OF THESE WHEN IT GAINS OR LOSES AN ELECTRON	$400	WHAT IS
IR"RESISTABLE" GERMAN PHYSICIST WITH A LAW ABOUT THE FLOW OF AN ELECTRIC CURRENT	$500	WHO WAS

JEOPARDY!

3-LETTER SCIENCE

$100	WHAT IS A BUD?	**$100**
$200	WHAT IS THE SUN?	**$200**
$300	WHAT IS TIN?	**$300**
$400	WHAT IS AN ION?	**$400**
$500	WHO WAS (GEORG SIMON) OHM?	**$500**

DOUBLE JEOPARDY!

ALL THE WORLD'S A STAGE

THIS CITY'S FAMED "ART THEATRE" OPENED IN 1898 WITH A PRODUCTION OF "CZAR FYODOR IVANOVICH"	**$200**	WHAT IS
THE 2-LETTER NAME OF THIS FORM OF JAPANESE DRAMA MEANS "TALENT" OR "SKILL"	**$400**	WHAT IS
SEVERAL OF HIS PLAYS, INCLUDING "LONG DAY'S JOURNEY INTO NIGHT", HAD THEIR WORLD PREMIERES IN STOCKHOLM	**$600**	WHO IS
THIS EXISTENTIALIST'S PLAY "THE FLIES", OR "LES MOUCHES", DEBUTED IN NAZI-OCCUPIED PARIS IN 1943	**$800**	WHO IS
THIS FAMED IRISH THEATRE THAT OPENED IN 1904 IS NAMED FOR THE STREET ON WHICH IT'S LOCATED	**$1000**	WHAT IS

DOUBLE JEOPARDY!

ALL THE WORLD'S A STAGE

$200	WHAT IS MOSCOW?	$200
$400	WHAT IS NO?	$400
$600	WHO IS EUGENE O'NEILL?	$600
$800	WHO IS JEAN-PAUL SARTRE?	$800
$1000	WHAT IS THE ABBEY THEATRE?	$1000

DOUBLE JEOPARDY!

THE CARIBBEAN

IN 1992 SANTO DOMINGO'S QUINTO CENTENARIO CELEBRATION HONORED THIS EXPLORER'S DISCOVERY	**$200**	WHO IS
EVERY AUGUST THIS COUNTRY IS HOME TO THE REGGAE SUNSPLASH	**$400**	WHAT IS
EL YUNQUE, THE ONLY TRULY TROPICAL RAIN FOREST IN THE U.S. NATIONAL FOREST SYSTEM, IS ON THIS ISLAND POSSESSION	**$600**	WHAT IS
IT'S T&T TO THE NATIVES BUT DESMOND TUTU CALLED THIS NATION THE RAINBOW COUNTRY	**$800**	WHAT IS
THE DUTCH SIDE OF THIS ISLAND USES 110 VOLTS; THE FRENCH SIDE, 220	**$1000**	WHAT IS

DOUBLE JEOPARDY!

THE CARIBBEAN

$200	WHO IS CHRISTOPHER COLUMBUS?	**$200**
$400	WHAT IS JAMAICA?	**$400**
$600	WHAT IS PUERTO RICO?	**$600**
$800	WHAT IS TRINIDAD & TOBAGO?	**$800**
$1000	WHAT IS ST. MARTIN?	**$1000**

94

DOUBLE JEOPARDY!

FIRST NAMES

JUDGE ITO, OR A WEAPON	**$200**	WHO IS
THE "HEAVENLY" MS. BASSETT	**$400**	WHO IS
A MIGHTY WARRIOR, LIKE FOOTBALL'S PAYTON	**$600**	WHO IS
DECEMBER-BORN PLAYWRIGHT COWARD	**$800**	WHO IS
"FLOWERY" NOVELIST MURDOCH	**$1000**	WHO IS

DOUBLE JEOPARDY!

FIRST NAMES

$200 — WHO IS LANCE? — $200

$400 — WHO IS ANGELA? — $400

$600 — WHO IS WALTER? — $600

$800 — WHO IS NOEL? — $800

$1000 — WHO IS IRIS? — $1000

DOUBLE JEOPARDY!

R.E.M.

THE LINEUP 1980–1997: GUITARIST PETER BUCK, BASSIST MIKE MILLS, DRUMMER BILL BERRY & THIS SINGER	**$200**	WHO IS
THIS R.E.M. SONG GAVE A 1999 JIM CARREY MOVIE ITS TITLE	**$400**	WHAT IS
IN 1988 R.E.M. SAID "THAT'S ALL FOLKS!" TO I.R.S. RECORDS & SIGNED WITH THIS LABEL FOR BIG BUCKS	**$600**	WHAT IS
THE VIDEO FOR THE SONG TITLED "LOSING" THIS WAS BANNED IN IRELAND	**$800**	WHAT IS
R.E.M. FOLLOWED "NEW ADVENTURES IN HI-FI" WITH THIS ALBUM THAT HAS A 2-LETTER TITLE	**$1000**	WHAT IS

DOUBLE JEOPARDY!

R.E.M.

$200	WHO IS MICHAEL STIPE?	$200
$400	WHAT IS "MAN ON THE MOON"?	$400
$600	WHAT IS WARNER BROS.?	$600
$800	WHAT IS "(LOSING) MY RELIGION"?	$800
$1000	WHAT IS "UP"?	$1000

DOUBLE JEOPARDY!

DISCOVERERS

Clue	Value	Response
IN THE 1570s THIS BRITISH CIRCUM-NAVIGATOR ATTACKED MANY SPANISH SHIPS AS A PIRATE IN THE CARIBBEAN	$200	WHO IS
THIS REAR ADMIRAL DISCOVERED A MOUNTAIN RANGE IN ANTARCTICA ON ONE OF HIS FAMOUS FLIGHTS OVER IT	$400	WHO IS
THIS MAN WHO SOUGHT THE SOURCE OF THE NILE WAS KNIGHTED IN 1886	$600	WHO IS
THIS PRIEST FIRST MET LOUIS JOLLIET WHEN JOLLIET ARRIVED AT HIS MISSION AT ST. IGNACE IN DECEMBER 1672	$800	WHO IS
IN 1497 THIS VENETIAN SAILING FOR ENGLAND BECAME THE FIRST EUROPEAN SINCE THE VIKINGS TO REACH N. AMERICA	$1000	WHO IS

DOUBLE JEOPARDY!

DISCOVERERS

$200	WHO IS SIR FRANCIS DRAKE?	$200
$400	WHO IS RICHARD EVELYN BYRD?	$400
$600	WHO IS SIR RICHARD FRANCIS BURTON?	$600
$800	WHO IS JACQUES MARQUETTE?	$800
$1000	WHO IS JOHN CABOT? (ACCEPT: GIOVANNI CABOTTO)	$1000

DOUBLE JEOPARDY!

HOMOPHONES

Clue	Value	Response
A CERTAIN CLOTHING ITEM, OR A TYPE OF ASIAN RESTAURANT THAT PROBABLY WON'T MAKE YOU WEAR ONE	$200	WHAT IS
IT'S WHAT'S NAMED FOR ZEBULON PIKE, OR THE BRIEF GLIMPSE HE GOT OF IT	$400	WHAT IS
WHAT HURRICANE ANDREW DID, OR HOW SOME PEOPLE FELT WHEN HE DID IT	$600	WHAT IS
A RED DEER, OR A BODY PART THAT MIGHT LEAP WHEN YOU SEE ONE	$800	WHAT IS
WHAT YOU DO TO A HOOK, OR WHAT YOU DO WITH YOUR BREATH WHILE WAITING FOR A FISH TO BITE	$1000	WHAT IS

DOUBLE JEOPARDY!

HOMOPHONES

$200	WHAT IS TIE/THAI?	$200
$400	WHAT IS PEEK/PEAK?	$400
$600	WHAT IS BLEW/BLUE?	$600
$800	WHAT IS A HART/HEART?	$800
$1000	WHAT IS BAIT/BATE?	$1000

FINAL JEOPARDY!
THE MOVIES

"A BOY'S LIFE" WAS THE
ORIGINAL TITLE OF THIS
1982 BLOCKBUSTER

WHAT IS

FINAL JEOPARDY!

THE MOVIES

WHAT IS "E.T.
(THE EXTRA-TERRESTRIAL)"?

JEOPARDY!

YANKEE INGENUITY

Clue	Value	Response
IT'S REPORTED THAT THE U.S. HAS ISSUED OVER 1870 PATENTS FOR THIS FLOWER; 400 OF THEM MENTION RED	$100	WHAT IS
THE MOTOR-DRIVEN PHONOGRAPH HE INVENTED IN 1888 PLAYED WAX CYLINDERS	$200	WHO IS
IN 1931 MILES LABORATORIES FIRST MARKETED THIS EFFERVESCENT TABLET	$300	WHAT IS
JOHN CURTIS MADE A SPRUCE-BASED TYPE IN 1848; THOMAS ADAMS MADE A CHICLE-BASED TYPE AROUND 1870	$400	WHAT IS
DU PONT SCIENTISTS ARE CREDITED WITH INVENTING THIS MATERIAL LATER USED TO DESCRIBE RONALD REAGAN & JOHN GOTTI	$500	WHAT IS

JEOPARDY!

YANKEE INGENUITY

$100   WHAT IS THE ROSE? $100

$200   WHO IS THOMAS EDISON? $200

$300   WHAT IS ALKA-SELTZER? $300

$400   WHAT IS CHEWING GUM? $400

$500   WHAT IS TEFLON? $500

JEOPARDY!

"ACE" IN THE HOLE

INDIANA'S NBA TEAM	**$100**	WHO ARE
A RHYTIDECTOMY; IT'S A NIP & TUCK DONE ON THE MUG	**$200**	WHAT IS
A SPIKED MEDIEVAL WEAPON, OR A SPRAY THAT CAN HAVE NEARLY THE SAME EFFECT	**$300**	WHAT IS
ONE GOES BETWEEN THE DINNER PLATE & THE DINNER TABLE	**$400**	WHAT IS
WHALES, DOLPHINS & PORPOISES	**$500**	WHAT ARE

JEOPARDY!™

"ACE" IN THE HOLE

$100	WHO ARE THE PACERS?	**$100**
$200	WHAT IS A FACE-LIFT?	**$200**
$300	WHAT IS MACE?	**$300**
$400	WHAT IS A PLACE MAT?	**$400**
$500	WHAT ARE CETACEANS? (ACCEPT: CETACEA)	**$500**

JEOPARDY!

A SUPREME CATEGORY

Clue	Value	Response
GIVING YOUR LIFE FIGHTING FOR YOUR COUNTRY IS THE SUPREME ONE; A BUNT IS A LESSER ONE	**$100**	WHAT IS
HE WAS SUPREME COMMANDER OF ALLIED FORCES IN EUROPE, & LATER OF NATO FORCES	**$200**	WHO IS
MISSOURI'S MOTTO "SALUS POPULI SUPREMA LEX ESTO" MEANS THE PEOPLE'S WELFARE SHALL BE THE SUPREME THIS	**$300**	WHAT IS
IN A C.S. FORESTER NOVEL, THIS BRITISH SEA CAPTAIN HAS TO DEAL WITH A CRAZED DICTATOR NAMED EL SUPREMO	**$400**	WHO IS
FROM THE 1930s TO THE 1980s IT WAS THE 2-CHAMBERED LEGISLATURE OF THE USSR	**$500**	WHAT IS

JEOPARDY!

A SUPREME CATEGORY

$100 — WHAT IS A SACRIFICE? — **$100**

$200 — WHO IS DWIGHT D. EISENHOWER? — **$200**

$300 — WHAT IS LAW? — **$300**

$400 — WHO IS HORATIO HORNBLOWER? — **$400**

$500 — WHAT IS THE SUPREME SOVIET? (SUPREME COUNCIL) — **$500**

JEOPARDY!

BLOOD TEST

Clue	Value	Response
PEOPLE WHO LIVE AT HIGH ALTITUDES OFTEN HAVE THICKER BLOOD, TO DELIVER MORE OF THIS GAS TO BODY CELLS	$100	WHAT IS
THROMBOSES & EMBOLISMS ARE COMMON CAUSES OF STROKES, THE INTERRUPTION OF THE BLOOD SUPPLY TO THIS ORGAN	$200	WHAT IS
IF THIS "FACTOR" DIFFERS IN A PREGNANT WOMAN & HER FETUS, THE BABY'S RED BLOOD CELLS MAY BE DAMAGED	$300	WHAT IS
DOCTORS ARE AGAIN USING THESE BLOOD-SUCKING WORMS, NOW TO REMOVE CLOTS IN FINGERS REATTACHED BY MICROSURGERY	$400	WHAT ARE
TYPE AB IS CONSIDERED THE UNIVERSAL RECIPIENT; THIS TYPE IS THE UNIVERSAL DONOR	$500	WHAT IS

JEOPARDY!

BLOOD TEST

$100 WHAT IS OXYGEN? **$100**

$200 WHAT IS THE BRAIN? **$200**

$300 WHAT IS THE RH FACTOR? **$300**

$400 WHAT ARE LEECHES? **$400**

$500 WHAT IS O? **$500**

JEOPARDY!

WOMEN'S WORK

Clue	Value	Response
IN 1977 KAY KOPLOVITZ FOUNDED WHAT BECAME THIS "PATRIOTIC" CABLE NETWORK, HOME TO "LA FEMME NIKITA"	$100	WHAT IS
THIS FUTURE SUPREME COURT JUSTICE HID HER PREGNANCY FOR FEAR OF LOSING HER TEACHING JOB AT RUTGERS	$200	WHO IS
THIS WOMAN NOT ONLY FOUNDED THE FIRST BIRTH CONTROL CLINIC, SHE ALSO PIONEERED THE TERM	$300	WHO IS
"AMERICA'S SWEET-HEART", SHE WAS JUST 24 IN 1917 WHEN SHE COMMANDED $350,000 PER FILM	$400	WHO IS
THIS LONGTIME WASHINGTON POST EDITOR & NEWSWEEK COMMENTATOR PASSED AWAY IN 1999	$500	WHO IS

JEOPARDY!

WOMEN'S WORK

$100 — WHAT IS THE USA NETWORK? — $100

$200 — WHO IS RUTH BADER GINSBURG? — $200

$300 — WHO IS MARGARET SANGER? — $300

$400 — WHO IS MARY PICKFORD? — $400

$500 — WHO IS MEG GREENFIELD? — $500

JEOPARDY!

1990s TELEVISION

Clue	Value	Response
FOX DRAMA ABOUT THE PLIGHT OF THE SALINGER CHILDREN, ORPHANED BY A CAR WRECK	$100	WHAT IS
THIS BILL MAHER GABFEST STARTED ON COMEDY CENTRAL & MOVED TO ABC	$200	WHAT IS
ROSLYN, WASHINGTON REPRESENTED CICELY, ALASKA, THE SETTING OF THIS ROB MORROW SERIES	$300	WHAT IS
THE QUIRKY DRAMA "PICKET FENCES" WAS SET IN THE TOWN OF ROME IN THIS STATE, NOT IN ITALY	$400	WHAT IS
"TWIN PEAKS" WAS THE FIRST TV VENTURE FOR THIS "ERASERHEAD" DIRECTOR	$500	WHO IS

JEOPARDY!

1990s TELEVISION

$100	WHAT IS "PARTY OF FIVE"?	**$100**
$200	WHAT IS "POLITICALLY INCORRECT"?	**$200**
$300	WHAT IS "NORTHERN EXPOSURE"?	**$300**
$400	WHAT IS WISCONSIN?	**$400**
$500	WHO IS DAVID LYNCH?	**$500**

DOUBLE JEOPARDY!

HAIL, HAIL ALBANIA

Clue	Value	Response
IN THIS 1997 DUSTIN HOFFMAN FILM, THE U.S. WAGES A FICTIONAL WAR WITH ALBANIA	$200	WHAT IS
ALBANIA IS LOCATED ON THE EASTERN SHORES OF THE IONIAN SEA & THIS SEA	$400	WHAT IS
ALBANIA'S CAPITAL, IT CENTERS ON SKANDERBEG SQUARE	$600	WHAT IS
AFTER ALBANIA BROKE WITH THE USSR, IT TURNED TO THIS COUNTRY WHICH GAVE IT BILLIONS UNTIL A TIFF IN 1978	$800	WHAT IS
KING ZOG I RULED FROM 1928 UNTIL 1939, WHEN THIS COUNTRY ANNEXED ALBANIA	$1000	WHAT IS

DOUBLE JEOPARDY!

HAIL, HAIL ALBANIA

$200 WHAT IS "WAG THE DOG"? **$200**

$400 WHAT IS THE ADRIATIC SEA? **$400**

$600 WHAT IS TIRANE? **$600**

$800 WHAT IS CHINA? **$800**

$1000 WHAT IS ITALY? **$1000**

DOUBLE JEOPARDY!

CONTEMPORARIES

BURNT AT THE STAKE IN 1431, SHE WAS PROBABLY A PIN-UP GIRL FOR 11-YEAR-OLD TORQUEMADA	**$200**	WHO IS
WHILE JAMES WATT WAS GETTING STEAMED UP IN SCOTLAND, SHE WAS HEATING UP THE THRONE IN RUSSIA	**$400**	WHO IS
WHILE MONTEZUMA WAS RULING THE AZTECS, THIS POLE WAS MOVING THE SUN OUT OF THE CENTER OF THE UNIVERSE	**$600**	WHO IS
WHILE LEIF ERICSON HAD HIS FIRST LOOK AT THE NEW WORLD, THIS MAN WAS SITTING AS FIRST KING OF HUNGARY	**$800**	WHO IS
IN 1850 HAWTHORNE WROTE OF HESTER PRYNNE'S CRIME & THIS SCOT OPENED HIS CHICAGO DETECTIVE AGENCY	**$1000**	WHO IS

DOUBLE JEOPARDY!

CONTEMPORARIES

$200	WHO IS JOAN OF ARC?	$200
$400	WHO IS CATHERINE THE GREAT? (ACCEPT: CATHERINE II)	$400
$600	WHO IS NICOLAUS COPERNICUS?	$600
$800	WHO IS (ST.) STEPHEN (I)?	$800
$1000	WHO IS ALLAN PINKERTON?	$1000

DOUBLE JEOPARDY!

LET'S PLAY POKER

THE 2 BASIC TYPES OF POKER ARE DRAW & THIS ONE WITH CARDS DEALT UP & DOWN	**$200**	WHAT IS
IT'S THE REGAL NAME FOR A TEN, JACK, QUEEN, KING & ACE ALL OF ONE SUIT	**$400**	WHAT IS
2-WORD NAME FOR THE NEXT HAND IN VALUE BELOW FOUR OF A KIND	**$600**	WHAT IS
MANY PLAYERS HAVE TRIED THEIR LUCK AT THE WORLD SERIES OF POKER HELD IN THIS LAS VEGAS CASINO	**$800**	WHAT IS
IT'S A SEQUENCE SUCH AS THE FOUR, SIX, SEVEN & EIGHT, NEEDING ONE TANTALIZING CARD TO FILL IT	**$1000**	WHAT IS

DOUBLE JEOPARDY!

LET'S PLAY POKER

$200	WHAT IS STUD? (ACCEPT: OPEN)	**$200**
$400	WHAT IS A ROYAL FLUSH?	**$400**
$600	WHAT IS A FULL HOUSE?	**$600**
$800	WHAT IS (BINION'S) HORSESHOE?	**$800**
$1000	WHAT IS AN INSIDE STRAIGHT?	**$1000**

DOUBLE JEOPARDY!

MOVIE ADAPTATIONS

THE 2-WORD TITLE OF THIS CARL HIAASEN NOVEL BECAME ONE WORD WHEN DEMI MOORE DISROBED ON FILM	**$200**	WHAT IS
THIS BOGART-BERGMAN FILM IS BETTER REMEMBERED THAN ITS SOURCE, THE PLAY "EVERYBODY COMES TO RICK'S"	**$400**	WHAT IS
KEVIN KLINE & JOAN ALLEN WERE MOODY INDEED IN THIS "CHILLING" 1997 DRAMA FROM A RICK MOODY NOVEL	**$600**	WHAT IS
THIS FILM ABOUT A DYING CATCHER, BASED ON A MARK HARRIS NOVEL, TOOK ITS TITLE FROM "THE STREETS OF LAREDO"	**$800**	WHAT IS
1951's "A PLACE IN THE SUN" ADAPTS THIS CLASSIC "AMERICAN" NOVEL BY THEODORE DREISER	**$1000**	WHAT IS

DOUBLE JEOPARDY!

MOVIE ADAPTATIONS

$200	WHAT IS "STRIP TEASE"?
$400	WHAT IS "CASABLANCA"?
$600	WHAT IS "THE ICE STORM"?
$800	WHAT IS "BANG THE DRUM SLOWLY"?
$1000	WHAT IS "AN AMERICAN TRAGEDY"?

DOUBLE JEOPARDY!

HOW SUITE IT IS

Clue	Value	Response
AROUND 1725 THIS GREAT BAROQUE COMPOSER WROTE 6 "ENGLISH SUITES" FOR HARPSICHORD	$200	WHO IS
WHEN YOU LISTEN TO THIS FRENCH COMPOSER'S "MOTHER GOOSE" SUITE, WEAR A "BOLERO"	$400	WHO IS
THIS COMPOSER'S "PEER GYNT" SUITES BEGAN LIFE AS INCIDENTAL MUSIC FOR A PLAY BY HENRIK IBSEN	$600	WHO IS
GROFE'S 1931 SUITE NAMED FOR THIS ARIZONA SITE IS A LANDMARK IN AMERICAN MUSIC	$800	WHAT IS
"FAR EAST SUITE" IS AN IMPORTANT WORK BY THIS "NOBLE" BANDLEADER	$1000	WHO IS

DOUBLE JEOPARDY!

HOW SUITE IT IS

$200	WHO IS JOHANN SEBASTIAN BACH?	**$200**
$400	WHO IS MAURICE RAVEL?	**$400**
$600	WHO IS EDVARD GRIEG?	**$600**
$800	WHAT IS THE "GRAND CANYON SUITE"?	**$800**
$1000	WHO IS DUKE ELLINGTON?	**$1000**

DOUBLE JEOPARDY!

EPONYMS

Clue	Value	Response
SCIENTIST LUIGI GALVANI INSPIRED THIS WORD THAT CAN MEAN "TO SHOCK INTO ACTION"	$200	WHAT IS
ALTHOUGH HE LED THE ILL-FATED CHARGE OF THE LIGHT BRIGADE, THIS EARL IS BEST KNOWN FOR HIS SWEATER	$400	WHO IS
A CRACKER IS NAMED FOR THIS DIETARY REFORMER WHO ADVOCATED USING UNSIFTED WHOLE WHEAT FLOUR	$600	WHO IS
MANY SCHOLARS BELIEVE "O.K." COMES FROM "OLD KINDER-HOOK", THIS PRESI-DENT'S NICKNAME	$800	WHO IS
THESE -ISMS ARE NAMED FOR A CLERGYMAN WHO REPORTEDLY SAID THAT BEING FORCED TO RETIRE "CAME AS A BLUSHING CROW"	$1000	WHAT ARE

DOUBLE JEOPARDY!

EPONYMS

$200	WHAT IS GALVANIZE?	**$200**
$400	WHO IS (THE EARL OF) CARDIGAN?	**$400**
$600	WHO IS (DR. SYLVESTER) GRAHAM?	**$600**
$800	WHO IS MARTIN VAN BUREN?	**$800**
$1000	WHAT ARE SPOONERISMS?	**$1000**

FINAL JEOPARDY!

PLAYS

BASED ON A MYTH,
THIS 1913 PLAY BECAME
A 1938 MOVIE, A 1956
STAGE MUSICAL & A 1964
MOVIE MUSICAL

WHAT IS

FINAL JEOPARDY!
PLAYS

WHAT IS "PYGMALION"?

JEOPARDY!

"N"ATIONS OF THE WORLD

MAKE A TREK TO UTRECHT & YOU'LL FIND YOURSELF IN THIS COUNTRY	$100	WHAT IS
ON THE FIRST MONDAY IN JUNE, THIS KIWI COUNTRY CELEBRATES THE QUEEN'S BIRTHDAY	$200	WHAT IS
THE PEOPLE OF THIS NATION HELPFULLY GAVE THEIR CAPITAL, MANAGUA, A NAME THAT RHYMES WITH THE COUNTRY	$300	WHAT IS
IT HAS A RAT NAMED FOR IT	$400	WHAT IS
IT BECAME FULLY INDEPENDENT OF SOUTH AFRICA MARCH 21, 1990	$500	WHAT IS

JEOPARDY!

"N"ATIONS OF THE WORLD

$100	WHAT IS THE NETHERLANDS?	**$100**
$200	WHAT IS NEW ZEALAND?	**$200**
$300	WHAT IS NICARAGUA?	**$300**
$400	WHAT IS NORWAY?	**$400**
$500	WHAT IS NAMIBIA?	**$500**

JEOPARDY!

PIG-OUT

ANGUAGELAY OKENSPAY ISTHAY AYWAY	**$100**	WHAT IS
THIS MUPPET WAS FEATURED IN HER OWN "GREAT LOVERS OF THE SILVER SCREEN" CALENDAR	**$200**	WHO IS
IN GERMAN THIS PROVERBIALLY FILTHY PLACE IS A "SCHWEINESTALL"	**$300**	WHAT IS
THIS PORCINE "GREEN ACRES" STAR WAS A REAL HAM; HE WON 2 PATSY AWARDS AS TV ANIMAL OF THE YEAR	**$400**	WHO IS
THE WALRUS SAID IT WAS TIME "TO TALK OF MANY THINGS", ABOUT "WHY THE SEA IS BOILING HOT AND WHETHER" THIS	**$500**	WHAT IS

JEOPARDY!™

PIG-OUT

$100 | WHAT IS PIG LATIN? | $100

$200 | WHO IS MISS PIGGY? | $200

$300 | WHAT IS A PIGSTY? | $300

$400 | WHO IS ARNOLD (ZIFFEL)? | $400

$500 | WHAT IS "PIGS HAVE WINGS"? | $500

JEOPARDY!

IN THE SPIRIT

FRENCH FOR "A SITTING", IT'S A MEETING AT WHICH A MEDIUM TRIES TO COMMUNICATE WITH THE DEAD	**$100**	WHAT IS
THIS SHERLOCK HOLMES CREATOR BECAME AN ADVOCATE OF SPIRITUALISM AFTER HIS SON DIED IN WWI	**$200**	WHO WAS
CONSTANCE BENNETT & CARY GRANT APPEARED & DISAPPEARED IN THIS 1937 FILM CLASSIC	**$300**	WHAT IS
ROSEANNE & MADONNA ARE AMONG THE STARS WHO'VE STUDIED THIS JEWISH MYSTICAL TRADITION	**$400**	WHAT IS
POSSIBLY INHABITED BY A PIANO-PLAYING GHOST, THE STANLEY HOTEL IN COLORADO INSPIRED THIS STEPHEN KING TALE	**$500**	WHAT IS

JEOPARDY!

IN THE SPIRIT

$100 WHAT IS A SEANCE? $100

$200 WHO WAS SIR ARTHUR CONAN DOYLE? $200

$300 WHAT IS "TOPPER"? $300

$400 WHAT IS KABBALAH? (ACCEPT: ZOHAR) $400

$500 WHAT IS "THE SHINING"? $500

JEOPARDY!

FIRST LADIES

SHE WAS FIRST LADY FOR 12 YEARS & 39 DAYS	**$100**	WHO IS
SHE ACTED AS A COVER FOR HER HUSBAND WHILE THE 1978 CAMP DAVID PEACE TALKS WENT ON LONGER THAN EXPECTED	**$200**	WHO IS
HER FIRST MARRIAGE WAS TO WILLIAM WARREN OF GRAND RAPIDS, MICHIGAN	**$300**	WHO IS
JULIA TYLER BEGAN THE CUSTOM OF HAVING THIS SONG PLAYED AS A PRESIDENTIAL GREETING	**$400**	WHAT IS
IDA WENT WITH THIS MAN, HER HUSBAND, TO BUFFALO, BUT WASN'T PRESENT AT THE EXPOSITION WHERE HE WAS SHOT	**$500**	WHO IS

JEOPARDY!™

FIRST LADIES

$100 | WHO IS ELEANOR ROOSEVELT? | $100

$200 | WHO IS ROSALYNN CARTER? | $200

$300 | WHO IS BETTY FORD? | $300

$400 | WHAT IS "HAIL TO THE CHIEF"? | $400

$500 | WHO IS WILLIAM McKINLEY? | $500

JEOPARDY!

PROVERBS

Clue	Value	Response
IT "MAKES A MAN HEALTHY, WEALTHY, AND WISE"	$100	WHAT IS
IN "THE WIZARD OF OZ", DOROTHY CLICKS HER HEELS & REPEATS THIS PROVERB BEFORE SHE'S WHISKED BACK TO KANSAS	$200	WHAT IS
IT "SELDOM KNOCKS TWICE", SO MAKE THE MOST OF IT	$300	WHAT IS
"BETTER THE FOOT SLIP THAN" THIS BODY PART	$400	WHAT IS
"MARRY IN HASTE, AND" DO THIS "AT LEISURE" (OR "IN RENO")	$500	WHAT IS

JEOPARDY!

PROVERBS

$100	WHAT IS "EARLY TO BED AND EARLY TO RISE"?
$200	WHAT IS "THERE'S NO PLACE LIKE HOME"?
$300	WHAT IS OPPORTUNITY?
$400	WHAT IS THE TONGUE?
$500	WHAT IS REPENT?

JEOPARDY!

COUNTRY MUSIC

IN 1980 THIS OCTOGENARIAN COMIC HIT THE COUNTRY CHARTS WITH "I WISH I WAS EIGHTEEN AGAIN"	**$100**	WHO IS
IT'S THE COUNTRY THAT COUNTRY STARS ANNE MURRAY & SHANIA TWAIN CAME FROM	**$200**	WHAT IS
ON HIS 1990 ALBUM "NO FENCES", HE SANG OF HAVING "FRIENDS IN LOW PLACES"	**$300**	WHO IS
SHEENA EASTON MADE IT TO THE COUNTRY CHARTS WHEN SHE DID THE DUET "WE'VE GOT TONIGHT" WITH THIS MAN	**$400**	WHO IS
A.P., SARA & MAYBELLE WERE THE HEART OF THIS, "THE FIRST FAMILY OF COUNTRY MUSIC"	**$500**	WHAT IS

JEOPARDY!

COUNTRY MUSIC

$100	**WHO IS GEORGE BURNS?**	$100
$200	**WHAT IS CANADA?**	$200
$300	**WHO IS GARTH BROOKS?**	$300
$400	**WHO IS KENNY ROGERS?**	$400
$500	**WHAT IS THE CARTER FAMILY?**	$500

DOUBLE JEOPARDY!

REVELATIONS

MAKE WAY! MODERN SCIENCE HAS REVEALED THAT THIS PLANET TRAVELS AROUND THE SUN AT ABOUT 68,000 MPH	**$200**	WHAT IS
IN 1962 RACHEL CARSON REVEALED THE DANGERS OF TOXIC POLLUTION TO A MASS AUDIENCE IN THIS BOOK	**$400**	WHAT IS
USING LITMUS PAPER WILL REVEAL THE ACIDITY & ALKALINITY OF A SOLUTION ON A SCALE FROM 1 TO THIS NUMBER	**$600**	WHAT IS
THIS GERMAN'S EXCAVATIONS OF TROY IN THE 1870s REVEALED THE HOMERIC LEGENDS WERE NOT COMPLETELY A MYTH	**$800**	WHO IS
GREEK FOR "HEAT WRITING", THIS TECHNIQUE REVEALS ABNORMAL TISSUE GROWTH BY STUDYING TEMPERATURE	**$1000**	WHAT IS

DOUBLE JEOPARDY!

REVELATIONS

$200	WHAT IS THE EARTH?	**$200**
$400	WHAT IS "SILENT SPRING"?	**$400**
$600	WHAT IS 14?	**$600**
$800	WHO IS HEINRICH SCHLIEMANN?	**$800**
$1000	WHAT IS THERMOGRAPHY?	**$1000**

DOUBLE JEOPARDY!

CHEESE, PLEASE

Clue	Value	Response
THIS MOST FAMOUS GREEK CHEESE IS SOMETIMES DESCRIBED AS "PICKLED" BECAUSE IT'S CURED IN BRINE	$200	WHAT IS
THIS TYPE OF GRATED CHEESE IS NAMED FOR ITALY'S CAPITAL	$400	WHAT IS
DE MEAUX IS A SUPERIOR TYPE OF THIS OOZING FRENCH CHEESE	$600	WHAT IS
THE "BABY" TYPE OF THIS DUTCH CHEESE, SIMILAR TO EDAM, IS USUALLY ENCASED IN RED WAX	$800	WHAT IS
SAMSOE IS A SWISS-STYLE COW'S MILK CHEESE NAMED FOR AN ISLAND IN THIS SCANDINAVIAN COUNTRY	$1000	WHAT IS

DOUBLE JEOPARDY!

CHEESE, PLEASE

$200	WHAT IS FETA?	$200
$400	WHAT IS ROMANO?	$400
$600	WHAT IS BRIE?	$600
$800	WHAT IS GOUDA?	$800
$1000	WHAT IS DENMARK?	$1000

DOUBLE JEOPARDY!

AMERICAN ARTISTS

BEFORE TURNING TO PAINTING IN HER 70s, SHE EMBROIDERED PICTURES ON CANVAS	$200	WHO IS
IN 1963 THIS "CHRISTINA'S WORLD" PAINTER BECAME THE FIRST ARTIST TO RECEIVE THE PRESIDENTIAL MEDAL OF FREEDOM	$400	WHO IS
HIS PORTRAITS OF GEORGE WASHINGTON INCLUDE ATHENAEUM, VAUGHAN & HANDSDOWNE TYPES	$600	WHO IS
MANY OF HIS FAMOUS SEASCAPES WERE SET AT HIS HOME IN PROUT'S NECK, MAINE	$800	WHO IS
HIS WEB SITE SHOWS "BRILLIANTLY COLORED, STUNNINGLY ENER-GETIC IMAGES OF SPORTING EVENTS"	$1000	WHO IS

DOUBLE JEOPARDY!

AMERICAN ARTISTS

$200	WHO IS GRANDMA MOSES? (ACCEPT: ANNA MARY ROBERTSON MOSES)	**$200**
$400	WHO IS ANDREW WYETH?	**$400**
$600	WHO IS GILBERT STUART?	**$600**
$800	WHO IS WINSLOW HOMER?	**$800**
$1000	WHO IS LEROY NEIMAN?	**$1000**

DOUBLE JEOPARDY!

FLAG-WAVING

Clue	Value	Response
THE GREEN FIELD ON THE FLAG OF BANGLADESH REPRESENTS THIS RELIGION	**$200**	WHAT IS
ALBANIA'S FLAG FEATURES A DOUBLE-HEADED ONE OF THESE BIRDS; AUSTRIA'S HAS JUST ONE HEAD	**$400**	WHAT IS
THIS COUNTRY'S COAT OF ARMS, SEEN ON ITS FLAG, DEPICTS A LEGENDARY AZTEC VISION	**$600**	WHAT IS
WANT TO KNOW WAT'S DEPICTED ON THIS COUNTRY'S FLAG? ANGKOR WAT, THAT'S WAT!	**$800**	WHAT IS
CONSTELLATION DEPICTED WITH 5 STARS ON THE FLAG OF WESTERN SAMOA	**$1000**	WHAT IS

DOUBLE JEOPARDY!

FLAG-WAVING

$200	WHAT IS ISLAM?	$200
$400	WHAT IS AN EAGLE?	$400
$600	WHAT IS MEXICO?	$600
$800	WHAT IS CAMBODIA?	$800
$1000	WHAT IS THE SOUTHERN CROSS? (ACCEPT: THE CRUX)	$1000

DOUBLE JEOPARDY!

FAMILIAR QUOTATIONS . . . IN 1800

Clue	Value	Response
THIS 1726 NOVEL REPORTED THAT THE EMPEROR'S LARGEST HORSES WERE "EACH ABOUT FOUR INCHES AND A HALF HIGH"	$200	WHAT IS
ON NOV. 10, 1770 VOLTAIRE PENNED, "IF GOD DID NOT EXIST, IT WOULD BE NECESSARY TO" DO THIS	$400	WHAT IS
THIS BRITISH LEXICOGRAPHER CALLED JOHN DRYDEN "THE FATHER OF ENGLISH CRITICISM"	$600	WHO IS
THIS "CLASSY" SWEDE WROTE, "TO LIVE BY MEDICINE IS TO LIVE HORRIBLY"	$800	WHO IS
IN 1762 ROUSSEAU LAMENTED, "MAN IS BORN FREE, AND EVERYWHERE HE IS IN" THESE	$1000	WHAT ARE

DOUBLE JEOPARDY!

FAMILIAR QUOTATIONS . . . IN 1800

$200	WHAT IS "GULLIVER'S TRAVELS"?	**$200**
$400	WHAT IS "INVENT HIM"?	**$400**
$600	WHO IS SAMUEL JOHNSON?	**$600**
$800	WHO IS CAROLUS LINNAEUS?	**$800**
$1000	WHAT ARE CHAINS?	**$1000**

DOUBLE JEOPARDY!

THE OLYMPICS

Clue	Value	Response
HELEN WILLS & STEFFI GRAF WERE CONSECUTIVE GOLD MEDALISTS IN THIS SPORT, 64 YEARS APART	$200	WHAT IS
ON FEB. 22, 1980 MIKE ERUZIONE SCORED THE WINNING GOAL AS THE U.S. BEAT THIS COUNTRY IN HOCKEY	$400	WHAT IS
IN 1992, AT AGE 13, CHINA'S FU MINGXIA WON THE WOMEN'S PLATFORM GOLD MEDAL IN THIS SPORT	$600	WHAT IS
IN 1904 AMERICAN THOMAS HICKS WON THIS RACE AFTER AN EMERGENCY DOSE OF BRANDY & STRYCHNINE PARTWAY THROUGH	$800	WHAT IS
IN 1998 HERMANN MAIER, KNOWN BY THIS ARNOLDIAN NICKNAME, GOT UP FROM A SKI CRASH TO WIN GOLD AT NAGANO	$1000	WHAT IS

DOUBLE JEOPARDY!

THE OLYMPICS

$200	WHAT IS (SINGLES) TENNIS?	**$200**
$400	WHAT IS THE USSR?	**$400**
$600	WHAT IS DIVING?	**$600**
$800	WHAT IS THE MARATHON?	**$800**
$1000	WHAT IS THE HERMINATOR?	**$1000**

FINAL JEOPARDY!

ACTORS & THEIR FILMS

THE TITLE OF RICHARD
BURTON'S LAST FEATURE
FILM, OR THE YEAR
IT WAS RELEASED

WHAT IS

FINAL JEOPARDY!

ACTORS & THEIR FILMS

WHAT IS "1984"?

JEOPARDY!

AUSTRALIA

AUSTRALIA BOASTS THE ONLY ALL-BLACK TYPE OF THIS OFTEN WHITE & GRACEFUL AQUATIC BIRD	**$100**	WHAT IS
THE GAME CALLED THE "AUSTRALIAN RULES" TYPE OF THIS IS PLAYED ON A FIELD UP TO 200 YARDS LONG WITH 4 POSTS AT EACH END	**$200**	WHAT IS
ONE OF AUSTRALIA'S BEST-KNOWN EXPORTS IS THIS MAN SEEN IN "CROCODILE DUNDEE" & IN SUBARU ADS	**$300**	WHO IS
THIS PARTY LED AUSTRALIA FROM 1983 TO 1996, WHILE A PARTY OF THE SAME NAME WAS BRITAIN'S OPPOSITION	**$400**	WHAT IS
5-LETTER NAME OF THE CAPITAL OF WESTERN AUSTRALIA, NAMED FOR A COUNTY IN SCOTLAND	**$500**	WHAT IS

JEOPARDY!

AUSTRALIA

$100	WHAT IS THE SWAN?	$100
$200	WHAT IS FOOTBALL?	$200
$300	WHO IS PAUL HOGAN?	$300
$400	WHAT IS THE LABOUR PARTY?	$400
$500	WHAT IS PERTH?	$500

JEOPARDY!

TASTE TREATS

Clue	Value	Response
U.S. CITY NOTED FOR ITS CREAM CHEESE & CHEESE STEAKS	$100	WHAT IS
ELMER DOOLIN BOUGHT THE RECIPE FOR THESE FRIED CORN MEAL CHIPS FOR $100 & BUILT AN EMPIRE	$200	WHAT ARE
THIS FORMER TALENT AGENT FOUNDED HIS COOKIE EMPIRE IN 1975, 2 YEARS BEFORE MRS. FIELDS	$300	WHO IS
IN 1989 THIS COMPANY INTRODUCED ITS SYMPHONY BAR	$400	WHAT IS
1948 SAW THE INTRODUCTION OF THIS BRAND, THE FIRST MAJOR U.S. AEROSOL FOOD PRODUCT	$500	WHAT IS

JEOPARDY!

TASTE TREATS

$100	WHAT IS PHILADELPHIA?	**$100**
$200	WHAT ARE FRITOS?	**$200**
$300	WHO IS FAMOUS (WALLY) AMOS?	**$300**
$400	WHAT IS HERSHEY'S?	**$400**
$500	WHAT IS REDDI-WIP?	**$500**

JEOPARDY!

REPORTERS

SPORTSWRITER GRANTLAND RICE WROTE THAT THE "GREAT SCORER" MARKS "NOT THAT YOU WON OR LOST" BUT THIS	**$100**	WHAT IS
DURING THE GULF WAR WOLF BLITZER'S BEAT FOR CNN WAS THIS BUILDING WHERE HE SAW ALL SIDES OF AN ISSUE, NOT JUST 5	**$200**	WHAT IS
HIS BOOK "ANOTHER CITY, NOT MY OWN" IS BASED ON HIS TIME COVERING THE SIMPSON TRIAL FOR VANITY FAIR	**$300**	WHO IS
ROSCOE WAS THE MIDDLE NAME OF THIS MAN KNOWN FOR HIS CALM RADIO REPORTAGE DURING WWII	**$400**	WHO IS
THIS KING OF GONZO JOURNALISM WROTE OF "FEAR AND LOATHING IN LAS VEGAS" & IN THE 1972 CAMPAIGN	**$500**	WHO IS

JEOPARDY!

REPORTERS

$100	WHAT IS "HOW YOU PLAYED THE GAME"?	**$100**
$200	WHAT IS THE PENTAGON?	**$200**
$300	WHO IS DOMINICK DUNNE?	**$300**
$400	WHO IS EDWARD R. MURROW?	**$400**
$500	WHO IS HUNTER S. THOMPSON?	**$500**

162

JEOPARDY!

CANINE PROVERBS

COMPLETES THE TIMELY PROVERB "EVERY DOG HAS . . ."	**$100**	WHAT IS
IN OTHER WORDS, "THERE'S NO WAY TO EDUCATE ONE ANCIENT CANINE IN UP-TO-DATE ACTIONS"	**$200**	WHAT IS
"DOGS THAT" DO THIS "AT A DISTANCE SELDOM BITE"	**$300**	WHAT IS
IN LATIN IT'S "QUI ME AMAT, AMAT ET CANEM MEAM"	**$400**	WHAT IS
"INTO THE MOUTH OF A BAD DOG OFTEN FALLS A GOOD" ONE OF THESE	**$500**	WHAT IS

JEOPARDY!

CANINE PROVERBS

$100	WHAT IS "HIS DAY"?	**$100**
$200	WHAT IS "YOU CAN'T TEACH AN OLD DOG NEW TRICKS"?	**$200**
$300	WHAT IS "BARK"?	**$300**
$400	WHAT IS "LOVE ME, LOVE MY DOG"?	**$400**
$500	WHAT IS A "BONE"?	**$500**

JEOPARDY!

SPACY POP MUSIC

Clue	Value	Response
IN 1979 STING & THIS GROUP WERE "WALKING ON THE MOON"	$100	WHAT IS
"SPACE ODDITY" WAS HIS FIRST U.S. TOP 10 HIT	$200	WHO IS
IN 1992 MEMBERS OF QUEEN HELD A TRIBUTE CONCERT FOR THIS LATE LEAD SINGER	$300	WHO IS
HE WAS BORN IN LIVERPOOL ON JULY 7, 1940	$400	WHO IS
PUBLIC ENEMY CALLED THEIR 1990 ALBUM "FEAR OF" THIS	$500	WHAT IS

JEOPARDY!

SPACY POP MUSIC

$100	WHAT IS THE POLICE?	**$100**
$200	WHO IS DAVID BOWIE?	**$200**
$300	WHO IS FREDDIE MERCURY?	**$300**
$400	WHO IS RINGO STARR?	**$400**
$500	WHAT IS "A BLACK PLANET"?	**$500**

JEOPARDY!

IT'S A GUY THING

GUYS LOVE THIS EYE-GOUGING COMEDY TEAM WHO STARTED IN VAUDEVILLE IN 1923 AS JUST A DUO	**$100**	WHO ARE
PROVERBIALLY, THEY'RE WHAT MEN HATE ASKING FOR, EVEN IF THEY END, "YOU CAN'T MISS IT"	**$200**	WHAT ARE
IT'S THE MAIN HOR-MONE PRODUCING MALE CHARACTERISTICS LIKE FACIAL HAIR & LOVE OF SPORTS CARS	**$300**	WHAT IS
IN 1990 COLORADO COACH BILL McCART-NEY FOUNDED THIS MOVEMENT OF CHRISTIAN MEN	**$400**	WHO ARE
THIS MAGAZINE CALLS ITSELF "THE BEST THING TO HAPPEN TO MEN SINCE WOMEN"	**$500**	WHAT IS

JEOPARDY!

IT'S A GUY THING

$100	WHO ARE THE THREE STOOGES?	$100
$200	WHAT ARE DIRECTIONS?	$200
$300	WHAT IS TESTOSTERONE?	$300
$400	WHO ARE THE PROMISE KEEPERS?	$400
$500	WHAT IS MAXIM?	$500

DOUBLE JEOPARDY!

CHARLES V

IN 1541 CHARLES LED A DOOMED NAVAL CAMPAIGN TO TAKE ALGIERS FROM THIS TURKISH EMPIRE	$200	WHAT IS
IN 1522 THIS MAN WROTE CHARLES THAT THE AZTECS "SAID THAT BY NO MEANS WOULD THEY GIVE THEMSELVES UP"	$400	WHO IS
IN 1530 CHARLES BECAME THE LAST OF THESE EMPERORS TO BE CROWNED BY A POPE	$600	WHAT IS
IN 1522 CHARLES INTRODUCED THIS SPANISH INSTITUTION TO THE NETHERLANDS TO PERSECUTE PROTESTANTS	$800	WHAT IS
CHARLES CONVENED THE DIET OF WORMS WHERE THIS MAN REFUSED TO RECANT HIS BELIEFS	$1000	WHO IS

DOUBLE JEOPARDY!

CHARLES V

$200   WHAT IS THE OTTOMAN EMPIRE? $200

$400   WHO IS HERNAN CORTES? (ACCEPT: HERNANDO CORTEZ) $400

$600   WHAT IS A HOLY ROMAN EMPEROR? $600

$800   WHAT IS THE INQUISITION? $800

$1000   WHO IS MARTIN LUTHER? $1000

DOUBLE JEOPARDY!

COMEDIES

IN 1998 THIS NBC SITCOM WITH JERRY, ELAINE, GEORGE & KRAMER SIGNED OFF THE NETWORK	**$200**	WHAT IS
THE '80s PUT LISA BONET & MALCOLM-JAMAL WARNER ON THE MAP AS 2 OF THIS COMEDIAN'S TV KIDS	**$400**	WHO IS
1997 FILM CONCERNING A CUTE DOG, A GAY ARTIST, AN EARTHY WAITRESS & A REALLY STRANGE AUTHOR	**$600**	WHAT IS
TITLE OF A RAY WALSTON SITCOM & A LATER CHRISTOPHER LLOYD MOVIE	**$800**	WHAT IS
LAST NAME OF FELICITY, HEATHER GRAHAM'S CHARACTER IN THE SECOND AUSTIN POWERS MOVIE— OH, BEHAVE!	**$1000**	WHAT IS

DOUBLE JEOPARDY!

COMEDIES

$200	WHAT IS "SEINFELD"?	**$200**
$400	WHO IS BILL COSBY?	**$400**
$600	WHAT IS "AS GOOD AS IT GETS"?	**$600**
$800	WHAT IS "MY FAVORITE MARTIAN"?	**$800**
$1000	WHAT IS SHAGWELL?	**$1000**

DOUBLE JEOPARDY!

SCIENCE & NATURE

FOUND IN EASTERN AUSTRALIA & TASMANIA, THIS MAMMAL'S SCIENTIFIC NAME MEANS "BIRD-SNOUT"	**$200**	WHAT IS
THIS METAL USED IN STORAGE BATTERIES IS REFINED MAINLY FROM A GRAY METALLIC ORE CALLED GALENA	**$400**	WHAT IS
THE RETINA HAS ABOUT 75 TO 150 MILLION RODS & ONLY ABOUT 7 MILLION OF THESE RECEPTOR CELLS	**$600**	WHAT ARE
THIS INERT GAS SYMBOLIZED Ar IS USED TO FILL LIGHT BULBS TO PREVENT THE TUNGSTEN FILAMENT FROM EVAPORATING	**$800**	WHAT IS
IN DIGITAL WATCHES, LCD STANDS FOR LIQUID CRYSTAL DISPLAY; LED STANDS FOR THIS	**$1000**	WHAT IS

DOUBLE JEOPARDY!

SCIENCE & NATURE

$200	WHAT IS THE (DUCK-BILLED) PLATYPUS?	**$200**
$400	WHAT IS LEAD?	**$400**
$600	WHAT ARE CONES?	**$600**
$800	WHAT IS ARGON?	**$800**
$1000	WHAT IS LIGHT-EMITTING DIODE? (ACCEPT: LIQUID ELEMENT DISPLAY)	**$1000**

DOUBLE JEOPARDY!

SCOTTISH LIT

THIS AUTHOR WHO DELIGHTED GENERATIONS WITH "PETER PAN" WAS SHORT, SHY & LONELY	**$200**	WHO IS
WITH "WAVERLEY" & "IVANHOE", HE ESTABLISHED THE GENRE OF THE HISTORICAL NOVEL	**$400**	WHO IS
THIS 1996 FILM ABOUT SCOTTISH DRUGGIES WAS BASED ON A NOVEL BY IRVINE WELSH	**$600**	WHAT IS
ROBERT LOUIS STEVENSON BASED THIS NOVEL ABOUT DAVID BALFOUR ON AN ACTUAL SCOTTISH CRIME	**$800**	WHAT IS
ONE OF THE FIRST MAJOR SCOTTISH POEMS WAS JOHN BARBOUR'S 1376 CHRONICLE OF THIS KING SOMETIMES CALLED "THE BRUCE"	**$1000**	WHO IS

DOUBLE JEOPARDY!

SCOTTISH LIT

$200	WHO IS (SIR) JAMES M. BARRIE?	$200
$400	WHO IS SIR WALTER SCOTT?	$400
$600	WHAT IS "TRAINSPOTTING"?	$600
$800	WHAT IS "KIDNAPPED"?	$800
$1000	WHO IS ROBERT BRUCE? (ACCEPT: ROBERT I)	$1000

DOUBLE JEOPARDY!

CELEBRITY EXES

IN HAPPIER TIMES, THIS COUPLE FOUNDED DESILU PRODUCTIONS	**$200**	WHO ARE
IN THE '60s BARBRA STREISAND WAS MARRIED TO THIS ACTOR; THEIR SON JASON APPEARED IN "THE PRINCE OF TIDES"	**$400**	WHO IS
EVERYTHING DIDN'T COME UP ROSES FOR ERNEST BORGNINE & THIS ENTERTAINER; THEY SEPARATED AFTER A MONTH	**$600**	WHO IS
THIS FORMER WIFE OF NEIL SIMON HAS APPEARED AS MARTIN CRANE'S GIRLFRIEND SHERRY ON "FRASIER"	**$800**	WHO IS
JOHN DEREK'S PARTNERS INCLUDED THIS BLONDE "DYNASTY" ACTRESS	**$1000**	WHO IS

DOUBLE JEOPARDY!

CELEBRITY EXES

$200	WHO ARE LUCILLE BALL & DESI ARNAZ?	**$200**
$400	WHO IS ELLIOTT GOULD?	**$400**
$600	WHO IS ETHEL MERMAN?	**$600**
$800	WHO IS MARSHA MASON?	**$800**
$1000	WHO IS LINDA EVANS?	**$1000**

DOUBLE JEOPARDY!

"WATER"

Clue	Value	Response
THIS POISONOUS VIPER IS ALSO CALLED A COTTONMOUTH	**$200**	WHAT IS
THIS SERIES OF MONET WORKS WAS PAINTED NEAR THE END OF HIS LIFE WHEN HE WAS ALMOST BLIND	**$400**	WHAT IS
THE 23rd PSALM SAYS THE LORD "MAKETH ME TO LIE DOWN IN GREEN PASTURES: HE LEADETH ME" BESIDE THESE	**$600**	WHAT ARE
IN 1970 SIMON & GARFUNKEL SANG, "LIKE" THIS "I WILL LAY ME DOWN"	**$800**	WHAT IS
THIS IRISH CITY FOUNDED BY VIKING RAIDERS IN THE 800s IS BEST KNOWN FOR ITS GLASSWARE	**$1000**	WHAT IS

DOUBLE JEOPARDY!

"WATER"

$200	WHAT IS A WATER MOCCASIN?	$200
$400	WHAT IS "WATER LILIES"?	$400
$600	WHAT ARE "THE STILL WATERS"?	$600
$800	WHAT IS "A BRIDGE OVER TROUBLED WATER"?	$800
$1000	WHAT IS WATERFORD?	$1000

FINAL JEOPARDY!

COUNTRIES OF THE WORLD

THE 3 MOST POPULOUS
COUNTRIES, THEY ADDED
UP TO AN ESTIMATED
2.4 BILLION PEOPLE
IN THE MID-'90s

WHAT ARE

FINAL JEOPARDY!
COUNTRIES OF THE WORLD

WHAT ARE CHINA,
INDIA & THE UNITED
STATES OF AMERICA?

JEOPARDY!

THE OCEAN

Clue	Value	Response
THE NORTH POLE SITS NEAR THE CENTER OF THIS OCEAN	$100	WHAT IS
THE 2 BODIES WHOSE GRAVITATIONAL PULL ON THE EARTH HAS THE GREATEST EFFECT ON OCEAN TIDES	$200	WHAT ARE
THERE ARE 3 MAJOR TYPES OF THESE STRUCTURES IN THE TROPICS: FRINGING, BARRIER & ATOLLS	$300	WHAT ARE
THE CYANEA, A TYPE OF THIS CREATURE SCIENTISTS CALL THE MEDUSA, MAY HAVE 100-FOOT-LONG TENTACLES & NOT ONE BONE	$400	WHAT IS
YOU CROSS IT GOING FROM MOGADISHU TO THE MALDIVES	$500	WHAT IS

JEOPARDY!

THE OCEAN

$100 | WHAT IS THE ARCTIC OCEAN? | $100

$200 | WHAT ARE THE SUN & THE MOON? | $200

$300 | WHAT ARE (CORAL) REEFS? | $300

$400 | WHAT IS A JELLYFISH? (ACCEPT: SCYPHOZOA; MEDUSA) | $400

$500 | WHAT IS THE INDIAN OCEAN? | $500

JEOPARDY!

TOOL TIME

Clue	Value	Response
HENRY F. PHILLIPS INVENTED A POPULAR TYPE OF THIS HAND TOOL	$100	WHAT IS
IT CAN WEAR DOWN METAL, SHAPE PLASTIC OR BE BAKED IN A CAKE FOR A PRISON INMATE	$200	WHAT IS
THIS TYPE OF HAMMER IS NAMED FOR A 2-PRONGED SIDE USED TO PULL NAILS OUT	$300	WHAT IS
A BRACE & BIT IS A SIMPLE TYPE OF THIS HAND TOOL	$400	WHAT IS
THE CARPENTER & TORPEDO TYPES OF THIS MEASURING TOOL USE BUBBLES AS INDICATORS	$500	WHAT ARE

JEOPARDY!

TOOL TIME

$100	WHAT IS A SCREWDRIVER?	**$100**
$200	WHAT IS A FILE? (ACCEPT: RASP)	**$200**
$300	WHAT IS A CLAW HAMMER?	**$300**
$400	WHAT IS A DRILL?	**$400**
$500	WHAT ARE LEVELS?	**$500**

JEOPARDY!

STATES' FIGHTS

WEST VIRGINIA BROKE FROM VIRGINIA AFTER THE LEGISLATURE VOTED FOR THIS IN 1861	**$100**	WHAT IS
CALIFORNIA & ARIZONA'S 40-YEAR DISPUTE OVER WATER RIGHTS TO THIS RIVER ENDED IN 1963	**$200**	WHAT IS
MAINE SPLIT FROM THIS STATE IN 1819 IN PROTEST OF HIGH TAXES, POOR ROADS & THE DISTANCE TO THE CAPITAL	**$300**	WHAT IS
IN 1998 NEW YORK & NEW JERSEY MADE THEIR ARGUMENTS BEFORE THE SUPREME COURT OVER THIS HISTORIC ISLAND	**$400**	WHAT IS
IN 1855 MANY MEN FROM THIS SLAVE STATE VOTED IN KANSAS, LEADING TO BLOODSHED ALONG THE BORDER	**$500**	WHAT IS

JEOPARDY!

STATES' FIGHTS

$100	WHAT IS SECESSION (FROM THE UNION)?	**$100**
$200	WHAT IS THE COLORADO RIVER?	**$200**
$300	WHAT IS MASSACHUSETTS?	**$300**
$400	WHAT IS ELLIS ISLAND?	**$400**
$500	WHAT IS MISSOURI?	**$500**

JEOPARDY!

SPORTS SCORES

ONE STROKE UNDER PAR ON A HOLE IN GOLF IS A BIRDIE; ONE STROKE OVER IS ONE OF THESE	**$100**	WHAT IS
IN FOOTBALL, THE DEFENSE EARNS THIS MANY POINTS BY TACKLING THE OPPOSING TEAM'S BALL CARRIER IN HIS OWN END ZONE	**$200**	WHAT IS
IN VOLLEYBALL, ONLY THE SIDE WHO DID THIS AT THE BEGINNING OF PLAY CAN SCORE A POINT	**$300**	WHAT IS
IN THE NBA, A SHOT FROM HALF COURT IS WORTH THIS MANY POINTS	**$400**	WHAT IS
IN TOURNAMENT DARTS, IT'S THE MOST POINTS A PLAYER CAN EARN ON ONE THROW; THE MOST FOR ONE TURN IS 180	**$500**	WHAT IS

JEOPARDY!

SPORTS SCORES

$100	WHAT IS A BOGEY?	$100
$200	WHAT IS 2?	$200
$300	WHAT IS SERVE?	$300
$400	WHAT IS 3?	$400
$500	WHAT IS 60?	$500

JEOPARDY!

THE "D.T."s

IT'S WHAT YOU HEAR WHEN THE ONE YOU'RE HUNG UP ON HANGS UP ON YOU	$100	WHAT IS
IN THE ARMY IT'S A RAPID MARCH OF 180 STEPS A MINUTE	$200	WHAT IS
THE NFL's JOE GREENE GOT MEAN FROM THIS POSITION	$300	WHAT IS
LONGTIME JOB OF RAWLEY FARNSWORTH, WHO WAS THANKED BY TOM HANKS IN HIS 1994 OSCAR ACCEPTANCE	$400	WHAT IS
GROUP OF FLORIDA ISLANDS NAMED FROM THE SPANISH FOR "TURTLES"	$500	WHAT ARE

JEOPARDY!

THE "D.T."s

$100   **WHAT IS A DIAL TONE?** $100

$200   **WHAT IS DOUBLE TIME?** $200

$300   **WHAT IS DEFENSIVE TACKLE?** $300

$400   **WHAT IS DRAMA TEACHER?** $400

$500   **WHAT ARE THE DRY TORTUGAS?** $500

JEOPARDY!

VERY MYSTERIOUS

YOU CAN FILL SOME LARGE SHOES IF YOU'RE THIS YETI RELATIVE THAT'S ALSO CALLED A SASQUATCH	$100	WHAT IS
THIS INFAMOUS POLYGON SUPPOSEDLY SUCKS UP PLANES & SHIPS WITHOUT A TRACE; DON'T FORGET YOUR SHORTS!	$200	WHAT IS
SOME INVESTIGATORS BELIEVE THAT THIS COY LASSIE MIGHT BE A PLESIOSAUR	$300	WHO IS
THE EXACT FUNCTION OF THIS MEGALITHIC MONUMENT NEAR SALISBURY, ENGLAND HAS BAFFLED SCHOLARS	$400	WHAT IS
THE LAST PROPHECY FROM THE VIRGIN MARY'S APPEARANCE IN THIS PORTUGUESE TOWN BECAME A PAPAL SECRET	$500	WHAT IS

JEOPARDY!

VERY MYSTERIOUS

$100	WHAT IS A BIGFOOT?	**$100**
$200	WHAT IS THE BERMUDA TRIANGLE?	**$200**
$300	WHO IS THE LOCH NESS MONSTER? (ACCEPT: NESSIE)	**$300**
$400	WHAT IS STONEHENGE?	**$400**
$500	WHAT IS FATIMA?	**$500**

DOUBLE JEOPARDY!

U.S. CITIES

Clue	Value	Response
IN 1965 NASA OPENED ITS $8 MILLION MISSION CONTROL CENTER IN THIS TEXAS CITY	$200	WHAT IS
NEIL SIMON'S EUGENE JEROME HAD THE "BLUES" IN THIS MISSISSIPPI CITY	$400	WHAT IS
THIS OHIO CITY ON THE OHIO RIVER HAS BEEN DUBBED THE "QUEEN CITY OF THE WEST"	$600	WHAT IS
THIS SOUTHERN STATE CAPITAL IS NAMED FOR AN ENGLISH COURTIER	$800	WHAT IS
YOU MIGHT STAY AT THE HOTEL DEL CORONADO TO VISIT THIS CITY'S WORLD-FAMOUS ZOO	$1000	WHAT IS

DOUBLE JEOPARDY!

U.S. CITIES

$200	WHAT IS HOUSTON? **$200**
$400	WHAT IS BILOXI? **$400**
$600	WHAT IS CINCINNATI? **$600**
$800	WHAT IS RALEIGH (NORTH CAROLINA)? **$800**
$1000	WHAT IS SAN DIEGO (CALIFORNIA)? **$1000**

DOUBLE JEOPARDY!

ACTS

ACT 2 OF THIS FARCE FINDS ALGERNON MONCRIEFF EARNESTLY PRETENDING TO BE ERNEST WORTHING	**$200**	WHAT IS
ACT 1 OF THIS PLAY INTRODUCES JUROR NO. 8, THE MAN WHO CONVINCES THE OTHER 11 TO RE-EXAMINE THE EVIDENCE	**$400**	WHAT IS
IN ACT 1 OF THIS PLAY, HAPPY COMPLAINS TO BIFF ABOUT THEIR FATHER'S DRIVING	**$600**	WHAT IS
FINALLY IN ACT 2, DR. DYSART SOLVES THE RIDDLE OF THE BLINDED HORSES IN THIS PETER SHAFFER MASTERPIECE	**$800**	WHAT IS
IN ACT 3 OF THIS IONESCO WORK, BERENGER'S LADYLOVE DAISY RUNS OFF TO JOIN A PACK OF HORNED PACHYDERMS	**$1000**	WHAT IS

DOUBLE JEOPARDY!

ACTS

$200	WHAT IS "THE IMPORTANCE OF BEING EARNEST"?	**$200**
$400	WHAT IS "12 ANGRY MEN"?	**$400**
$600	WHAT IS "DEATH OF A SALESMAN"?	**$600**
$800	WHAT IS "EQUUS"?	**$800**
$1000	WHAT IS "RHINOCEROS"?	**$1000**

DOUBLE JEOPARDY!

FRUIT

Clue	Value	Response
ABOUT 50% OF THE U.S. ORANGE CROP IS OF THIS VARIETY THAT SHARES ITS NAME WITH A SPANISH CITY	**$200**	WHAT IS
THE BLACK SEEDS IN A PAPAYA MAY BE GROUND & USED LIKE THIS SPICE	**$400**	WHAT IS
ROLL THIS PERSIAN "FRUIT OF MANY SEEDS" ON THE TABLE & INSERT A STRAW THROUGH THE SKIN TO DRINK ITS JUICE	**$600**	WHAT IS
WHAT AMERICANS CALL THIS IS ACTUALLY AN ORANGE-FLESHED MUSKMELON	**$800**	WHAT IS
THIS FRUIT'S ORIGINS INCLUDE PORTUGAL FOR THE ROCHA, FRANCE FOR THE ANJOU & BELGIUM FOR THE BOSC	**$1000**	WHAT IS

DOUBLE JEOPARDY!

FRUIT

$200	WHAT IS VALENCIA?	**$200**
$400	WHAT IS PEPPER?	**$400**
$600	WHAT IS A POMEGRANATE?	**$600**
$800	WHAT IS A CANTALOUPE?	**$800**
$1000	WHAT IS THE PEAR?	**$1000**

DOUBLE JEOPARDY!

SCULPTURE

Clue	Value	Response
THIS ARTIST'S "THE THINKER" WAS ORIGINALLY INTENDED TO CROWN HIS "GATES OF HELL" MONUMENT	$200	WHO IS
ALEXANDER CALDER CALLED THESE CREATIONS "FOUR-DIMENSIONAL DRAWINGS"	$400	WHAT ARE
THIS COUNTRY'S SCULPTOR UNKEI IS RENOWNED FOR HIS WOODEN STATUES CARVED FOR BUDDHIST TEMPLES	$600	WHAT IS
IT FOLLOWS "BAS" IN A TERM FOR SCULPTURE WITH AN IMAGE IS SLIGHTLY RAISED ABOVE A FLAT SURFACE	$800	WHAT IS
A STATUE OF THIS COWBOY PAINTER & SCULPTOR REPRE-SENTS MONTANA IN THE U.S. CAPITOL'S STATUARY HALL	$1000	WHO IS

DOUBLE JEOPARDY!

SCULPTURE

$200 WHO IS AUGUSTE RODIN? **$200**

$400 WHAT ARE MOBILES? **$400**

$600 WHAT IS JAPAN? **$600**

$800 WHAT IS RELIEF? **$800**

$1000 WHO IS CHARLES MARION RUSSELL? **$1000**

DOUBLE JEOPARDY!

DEATH SENTENCES

APPROACHING ANOTHER CAR NEAR PASO ROBLES, CA. IN 1955, HIS LAST WORDS WERE "THAT GUY'S GOTTA SEE US"	**$200**	WHO IS
HE ASKED "WHO IS IT?" JUST BEFORE PAT GARRETT SHOT HIM	**$400**	WHO IS
JUST BEFORE THE END, THIS WELSH POET BOASTED, "I'VE HAD 18 STRAIGHT WHISKIES; I THINK THAT'S THE RECORD"	**$600**	WHO IS
SPEAKING OF HIS MISTRESS, THIS ENGLISH KING'S LAST REQUEST WAS "LET NOT POOR NELLY STARVE"	**$800**	WHO IS
JUST BEFORE "DEATH KINDLY STOPPED FOR" HER, THIS POET SIGHED, "I MUST GO IN; THE FOG IS RISING"	**$1000**	WHO IS

DOUBLE JEOPARDY!

DEATH SENTENCES

$200   WHO IS JAMES DEAN? $200

$400   WHO IS BILLY THE KID? $400

$600   WHO IS DYLAN THOMAS? $600

$800   WHO IS CHARLES II? $800

$1000   WHO IS EMILY DICKINSON? $1000

DOUBLE JEOPARDY!

FILM STARS

AFTER DIVORCING ROBERT WALKER, JENNIFER JONES MARRIED THIS "GONE WITH THE WIND" PRODUCER IN 1949	**$200**	WHO IS
IN "MAGNOLIA" THIS "MISSION: IMPOSSIBLE" STAR RAN A SEMINAR FOR MEN CALLED "SEDUCE AND DESTROY"	**$400**	WHO IS
AN OSCAR WINNER FOR "GOODFELLAS", HE ONCE PLAYED GUITAR FOR JOEY DEE & THE STARLITERS	**$600**	WHO IS
ELLEN MUST HAVE BEEN BURSTYN WITH PRIDE WHEN SHE WON AN OSCAR FOR THIS 1974 ROAD MOVIE	**$800**	WHAT IS
LATER A TALK SHOW HOST FOR CNBC, HE WAS CONSIDERED FOR THE RICHARD DREYFUSS ROLE IN "JAWS"	**$1000**	WHO IS

DOUBLE JEOPARDY!

FILM STARS

$200	WHO IS DAVID O. SELZNICK?
$400	WHO IS TOM CRUISE?
$600	WHO IS JOE PESCI?
$800	WHAT IS "ALICE DOESN'T LIVE HERE ANYMORE"?
$1000	WHO IS CHARLES GRODIN?

FINAL JEOPARDY!

BIBLICAL PEOPLE

HE'S THE FIRST PERSON
WHOSE DEATH IS
MENTIONED IN THE
BOOK OF EXODUS

WHO IS

FINAL JEOPARDY!

BIBLICAL PEOPLE

WHO IS JOSEPH?

JEOPARDY!

BODY WORKS

Clue	Value	Response
BREATHE EASY—YOUR RIGHT ONE OF THESE HAS 3 LOBES & YOUR LEFT HAS 2	**$100**	WHAT ARE
IT'S THE HINGE-LIKE JOINT THAT ALLOWS THE FOOT TO MOVE UP & DOWN	**$200**	WHAT IS
YOU HAVE 8 OF THESE TEETH, SOME OF WHICH MAY BE BUCK	**$300**	WHAT ARE
THIS PAIR OF TISSUE MASSES THAT CAN CAUSE SNORING LIES ABOVE THE TONSILS IN THE NASAL PASSAGE	**$400**	WHAT ARE
THE ELASTIC TYPE OF THIS CONNECTIVE TISSUE IS FOUND IN THE OUTER PART OF YOUR EAR	**$500**	WHAT IS

JEOPARDY!

BODY WORKS

$100 WHAT ARE YOUR LUNGS? **$100**

$200 WHAT IS THE ANKLE? **$200**

$300 WHAT ARE INCISORS? (ACCEPT: FRONT TEETH) **$300**

$400 WHAT ARE THE ADENOIDS? **$400**

$500 WHAT IS CARTILAGE? **$500**

JEOPARDY!

AUTHORS & THEIR SLEUTHS

HE CREATED MIKE HAMMER & PLAYED THE PART IN THE 1963 FILM "THE GIRL HUNTERS"	**$100**	WHO IS
IN THIS WILKIE COLLINS NOVEL, SERGEANT CUFF SEARCHES FOR THE MISSING TITLE DIAMOND	**$200**	WHAT IS
TITLE OCCUPATION OF CALEB CARR'S DR. LASZLO KREIZLER	**$300**	WHAT IS
THE INITIALS IN THE NAME OF THIS CREATOR OF DETECTIVE ADAM DALGLIESH DON'T STAND FOR "POLICE DEPARTMENT"	**$400**	WHO IS
MICHAEL HARRISON WROTE STORIES FEATURING THIS SLEUTH CREATED BY EDGAR ALLAN POE	**$500**	WHO IS

JEOPARDY!

AUTHORS & THEIR SLEUTHS

$100	WHO IS MICKEY SPILLANE?	**$100**
$200	WHAT IS "THE MOONSTONE"?	**$200**
$300	WHAT IS AN ALIENIST?	**$300**
$400	WHO IS P.D. JAMES?	**$400**
$500	WHO IS C. AUGUSTE DUPIN?	**$500**

JEOPARDY!

POTENT POTABLES

THE FERMENTED DRINK CALLED PERRY IS THE PEAR-BASED COUNTERPART OF THIS "HARD" APPLE DRINK	**$100**	WHAT IS
A BRAND OF GIN DISTILLED IN LONDON SHARES ITS NAME WITH THESE TOWER OF LONDON GUARDS	**$200**	WHAT ARE
IT'S COFFEE MIXED WITH WHISKEY, SUCH AS JAMESON'S, & TOPPED WITH WHIPPED CREAM	**$300**	WHAT IS
IT'S CALLED STOLI FOR SHORT	**$400**	WHAT IS
TRADER VIC CLAIMED CREDIT FOR INVENTING THIS RUM DRINK & SAID IT WAS NAMED BY A TAHITIAN FRIEND	**$500**	WHAT IS

JEOPARDY!

POTENT POTABLES

$100	WHAT IS CIDER?	$100
$200	WHAT ARE BEEFEATERS?	$200
$300	WHAT IS IRISH COFFEE?	$300
$400	WHAT IS STOLICHNAYA (VODKA)?	$400
$500	WHAT IS A MAI TAI?	$500

JEOPARDY!

STUPID ANSWERS

SEVENTEEN MAGAZINE SAYS IF YOU CAN'T AFFORD TO BUY A STAIRMASTER & YOUR HOUSE HAS THESE, USE THEM	**$100**	WHAT ARE
NAME OF THE HOTEL & OFFICE COMPLEX WHERE THE WATERGATE BREAK-IN OCCURRED	**$200**	WHAT IS
JESSE JACKSON JR. HAS A MASTERS DEGREE IN THIS FROM THE CHICAGO THEOLOGICAL SEMINARY	**$300**	WHAT IS
2 CIVIL WAR FORTS WERE BUILT ON THIS WESTERN ISLAND OF THE FLORIDA KEYS	**$400**	WHAT IS
IT'S THE CRY OF THE CHACHALACA BIRD OF SOUTH AMERICA	**$500**	WHAT IS

JEOPARDY!

STUPID ANSWERS

$100   WHAT ARE STAIRS? $100

$200   WHAT IS WATERGATE? $200

$300   WHAT IS THEOLOGY? $300

$400   WHAT IS KEY WEST? $400

$500   WHAT IS "CHACHALACA"? $500

JEOPARDY!

AROUND THE WORLD

YOU'LL FIND GREECE'S PARLIAMENT BUILDING ON SYNTAGMA SQUARE IN THIS CAPITAL	**$100**	WHAT IS
THE NAME OF THIS SOUTH AFRICAN PROVINCE MEANS "ACROSS THE VAAL"— THE VAAL RIVER, THAT IS	**$200**	WHAT IS
THIS COUNTRY'S CATHEDRAL OF LEON IS NOTED FOR ITS SOARING SPIRES & STAINED GLASS WINDOWS	**$300**	WHAT IS
THIS CAPITAL OF MALAYSIA LIES AT THE CONFLUENCE OF THE KLANG & GOMBAK RIVERS	**$400**	WHAT IS
THIS CARIBBEAN GROUP OF ISLANDS SHARES ITS NAME WITH AN ANIMAL RESEMBLING AN ALLIGATOR	**$500**	WHAT ARE

JEOPARDY!

AROUND THE WORLD

$100	WHAT IS ATHENS?
$200	WHAT IS THE TRANSVAAL?
$300	WHAT IS SPAIN?
$400	WHAT IS KUALA LUMPUR?
$500	WHAT ARE THE CAYMAN ISLANDS?

JEOPARDY!

MOVIE DEBUTS

SHE DEBUTED IN A BIT PART AS WOODY ALLEN'S DATE IN "ANNIE HALL" 2 YEARS BEFORE "ALIEN" MADE HER A STAR	**$100**	WHO IS
THIS HALF-SISTER OF COUNTRY SINGER WYNONNA FIRST HIT THE BIG SCREEN IN THE 1992 COMEDY "KUFFS"	**$200**	WHO IS
AT 13 THIS ACTRESS WITH A WEEKDAY IN HER NAME STARRED IN THE 1956 CLASSIC "ROCK, ROCK, ROCK!"	**$300**	WHO IS
THE AL PACINO LEGAL DRAMA ". . . AND JUSTICE FOR ALL" MARKED THE SCREEN DEBUT OF THIS ACTOR, LATER TV's "COACH"	**$400**	WHO IS
THIS SON OF COLLEEN DEWHURST & GEORGE C. SCOTT DEBUTED IN THE 1988 FILM "FIVE CORNERS"	**$500**	WHO IS

JEOPARDY!™

MOVIE DEBUTS

$100	WHO IS SIGOURNEY WEAVER?	**$100**
$200	WHO IS ASHLEY JUDD?	**$200**
$300	WHO IS TUESDAY WELD?	**$300**
$400	WHO IS CRAIG T. NELSON?	**$400**
$500	WHO IS CAMPBELL SCOTT?	**$500**

DOUBLE JEOPARDY!

LONG LIVE THE KING

JOHN HANCOCK SIGNED HIS NAME BIG SO "JOHN BULL", INCLUDING THIS KING, COULD READ IT WITHOUT GLASSES	**$200**	WHO IS
WHILE MARRIED TO ISABELLA, THIS 15th CENTURY MONARCH SIRED AT LEAST 2 DAUGHTERS WITH OTHER WOMEN	**$400**	WHO IS
AS HARPSICHORDIST FOR THIS PRUSSIAN KING, CARL PHILIPP EMANUEL BACH OFTEN ACCOMPANIED HIM IN CONCERT	**$600**	WHO IS
IN 1993 HE SUCCEEDED HIS BROTHER BAUDOUIN TO BECOME THE SIXTH KING OF THE BELGIANS	**$800**	WHO IS
PEDRO I, EMPEROR OF BRAZIL, WAS THE SON OF KING JOHN VI OF THIS COUNTRY	**$1000**	WHAT IS

DOUBLE JEOPARDY!

LONG LIVE THE KING

$200	WHO IS GEORGE III?	**$200**
$400	WHO IS FERDINAND?	**$400**
$600	WHO IS FREDERICK THE GREAT? (ACCEPT: FREDERICK II)	**$600**
$800	WHO IS ALBERT (II)?	**$800**
$1000	WHAT IS PORTUGAL?	**$1000**

DOUBLE JEOPARDY!

WALL PAINTERS

THIS "DRIPPER", WHO PAINTED ON THE FLOOR, WAS A STUDENT OF MISSOURI MURALIST THOMAS HART BENTON	**$200**	WHO IS
AT AGE 4 IN GUANAJUATO, MEXICO, HE WAS ALREADY DRAWING ON THE WALLS	**$400**	WHO IS
IN 1892 THE WORLD'S COLUMBIAN EXPO IN CHICAGO HIRED THIS WOMAN IMPRESSIONIST TO PAINT A MURAL	**$600**	WHO IS
THIS "THIRD OF MAY" ARTIST COVERED THE WALLS OF HIS COUNTRY HOUSE IN GROTESQUE PAINTINGS	**$800**	WHO IS
STUART DAVIS' MURAL FOR THIS ROOM IN ROCKEFELLER CENTER WAS TITLED "MURAL (MEN WITHOUT WOMEN)"	**$1000**	WHAT IS

DOUBLE JEOPARDY!

WALL PAINTERS

$200 · WHO IS JACKSON POLLOCK? · $200

$400 · WHO IS DIEGO RIVERA? · $400

$600 · WHO IS MARY CASSATT? · $600

$800 · WHO IS FRANCISCO GOYA? · $800

$1000 · WHAT IS THE MEN'S ROOM? · $1000

DOUBLE JEOPARDY!

MEMORABLE TV

Clue	Value	Response
SHOW ON WHICH YOU'D SEE CESAR ROMERO AS THE JOKER & DAVID WAYNE AS THE MAD HATTER	**$200**	WHAT IS
SHOW THAT GAVE US THE CATCH PHRASES "YOU BET YOUR BIPPY" & "HERE COME DE JUDGE"	**$400**	WHAT IS
MANY THOUGHT THE REAL STAR OF THIS '80s SERIES WAS A CAR CALLED THE GENERAL LEE	**$600**	WHAT IS
DR. KILDARE & THIS VINCE EDWARDS DOCTOR BEGAN PRACTICING ON TV IN 1961 & BOTH LEFT IN 1966	**$800**	WHO IS
HE SMOLDERED AS LANCE CUMSON ON "FALCON CREST"	**$1000**	WHO IS

DOUBLE JEOPARDY!

MEMORABLE TV

$200	WHAT IS "BATMAN"?	**$200**
$400	WHAT IS "(ROWAN & MARTIN'S) LAUGH-IN"?	**$400**
$600	WHAT IS "THE DUKES OF HAZZARD"?	**$600**
$800	WHO IS BEN CASEY?	**$800**
$1000	WHO IS LORENZO LAMAS?	**$1000**

DOUBLE JEOPARDY!

AT GREAT LENGTHS

TYPE OF "MILE" EQUAL TO 1 KNOT OR 1 MEAN MINUTE OF ARC ON THE MERIDIAN	**$200**	WHAT IS
THIS DISTANCE USED IN ASTRONOMY IS ABBREVIATED pc & IS EQUAL TO 19.2 TRILLION MILES	**$400**	WHAT IS
USED IN TAKING SOUNDINGS, IT EQUALS EXACTLY 6 FEET	**$600**	WHAT IS
IN THE 1968 OLYMPICS HE LONG-JUMPED AN AMAZING 29 FEET, 2 1/2 INCHES	**$800**	WHO IS
IT USUALLY EQUALED 3 MILES, SO THOSE FABLED BOOTS WOULD COVER 21 MILES	**$1000**	WHAT IS

DOUBLE JEOPARDY!

AT GREAT LENGTHS

$200   WHAT IS A NAUTICAL MILE? $200

$400   WHAT IS A PARSEC? $400

$600   WHAT IS A FATHOM? $600

$800   WHO IS BOB BEAMON? $800

$1000   WHAT IS A LEAGUE? $1000

DOUBLE JEOPARDY!

OFFICIAL STATE SEALS

THIS STATE'S SEAL FEATURES 2 CORNU-COPIAS, ONE CONTAINING A COUPLE OF SPUDS	**$200**	WHAT IS
THE REVERSE SIDE OF ITS SEAL CONTAINS THE 6 FLAGS OF THE NATIONS THAT ONCE RULED IT	**$400**	WHAT IS
NEW JERSEY'S SEAL SHOWS 3 PLOWS ON A SHIELD HELD BY LIBERTY & THIS ROMAN GODDESS OF AGRICULTURE	**$600**	WHO IS
ITS SEAL WAS CREATED IN 1905 FOR A PROPOSED STATE OF SEQUOYAH ENCOMPASSING 5 INDIAN REPUBLICS	**$800**	WHAT IS
A SEMINOLE WOMAN CAN BE SEEN ON ITS SEAL SPREADING FLOWERS ALONG THE SHORE	**$1000**	WHAT IS

DOUBLE JEOPARDY!
OFFICIAL STATE SEALS

$200	WHAT IS IDAHO?	**$200**
$400	WHAT IS TEXAS?	**$400**
$600	WHO IS CERES?	**$600**
$800	WHAT IS OKLAHOMA?	**$800**
$1000	WHAT IS FLORIDA?	**$1000**

DOUBLE JEOPARDY!

HEARD IN THE '80s

IN "SUDDEN IMPACT", CLINT EASTWOOD TOLD A BAD GUY, "GO AHEAD", DO THIS	**$200**	WHAT IS
"BORKING", CLOSE SCRUTINY, WAS HEARD AFTER ROBERT BORK'S FAILED NOMINATION TO THIS BODY	**$400**	WHAT IS
MARGARET THATCHER SAID OF THIS SOVIET LEADER, "WE CAN DO BUSINESS TOGETHER"	**$600**	WHO IS
AFTER BEING SHOT, RONALD REAGAN QUOTED JACK DEMPSEY'S "I FORGOT TO" DO THIS	**$800**	WHAT IS
IN 1986 DAN RATHER WAS ASSAULTED BY THUGS CALLING HIM "KENNETH" & ASKING THIS	**$1000**	WHAT IS

DOUBLE JEOPARDY!

HEARD IN THE '80s

$200	WHAT IS "MAKE MY DAY"?	$200
$400	WHAT IS THE U.S. SUPREME COURT?	$400
$600	WHO IS MIKHAIL GORBACHEV?	$600
$800	WHAT IS DUCK?	$800
$1000	(WHAT IS) WHAT'S THE FREQUENCY?	$1000

FINAL JEOPARDY!

CLASSICAL COMPOSERS

ONE OF HIS MOST FAMOUS
WORKS HAD ITS PREMIERE
ON A BARGE IN 1717

WHO IS

FINAL JEOPARDY!

CLASSICAL COMPOSERS

WHO IS
GEORGE FRIDERIC HANDEL?

JEOPARDY!

STATE CAPITALS

Clue	Value	Response
THIS NEW YORK CAPITAL WAS ONCE KNOWN AS BEVERWYCK	$100	WHAT IS
IN 1982 ALASKANS REJECTED A PROPOSAL THAT WOULD HAVE MADE WILLOW THE CAPITAL INSTEAD OF THIS CITY	$200	WHAT IS
IN HOPES THAT GERMANY WOULD HELP FINANCE ITS RAILROAD, NORTH DAKOTA NAMED ITS CAPITAL THIS	$300	WHAT IS
BUILT IN 1610, THE SPANISH PALACE OF GOVERNORS IN THIS SOUTHWEST CAPITAL IS NOW A MUSEUM	$400	WHAT IS
IT'S "THE BIRTHPLACE OF DIXIE"	$500	WHAT IS

JEOPARDY!

STATE CAPITALS

$100	WHAT IS ALBANY?	**$100**
$200	WHAT IS JUNEAU?	**$200**
$300	WHAT IS BISMARCK?	**$300**
$400	WHAT IS SANTA FE (NEW MEXICO)?	**$400**
$500	WHAT IS MONTGOMERY (ALABAMA)?	**$500**

JEOPARDY!

COW-ARDICE

LAST NAME OF THE WOMAN WHOSE COW ALLEGEDLY STARTED THE GREAT CHICAGO FIRE	**$100**	WHAT IS
MILKY-WHITE WAS THE NAME OF THE COW THAT THIS FICTIONAL KID SOLD FOR BEANS	**$200**	WHO IS
ELSIE, THIS DAIRY COMPANY'S COW SYMBOL, FIRST APPEARED LIVE AT THE 1939 WORLD'S FAIR	**$300**	WHAT IS
MRS. WIGGINS IS THE COW BUDDY OF FREDDY, A HEROIC ONE OF THESE ANIMALS IN BOOKS BY WALTER R. BROOKS	**$400**	WHAT IS
ANCIENT PEOPLE WHOSE GODDESS HATHOR HAD THE HEAD OF A COW	**$500**	WHO ARE

JEOPARDY!

COW-ARDICE

$100 — WHAT IS O'LEARY? — $100

$200 — WHO IS JACK? — $200

$300 — WHAT IS BORDEN? — $300

$400 — WHAT IS A PIG? — $400

$500 — WHO ARE THE EGYPTIANS? — $500

JEOPARDY!

MEDICAL KNOWLEDGE

Clue	Value	Response
IT'S BEEN JOKINGLY SAID OF THIS SPECIALTY THAT TREATS SKIN DISORDERS, "1,000 CONDITIONS; 2 CREAMS"	**$100**	WHAT IS
IN 1816 FRENCH PHYSICIAN RENE LAENNEC INVENTED THIS DEVICE USED TO LISTEN TO THE HEART & LUNGS	**$200**	WHAT IS
IN 1895 THIS SCIENTIST COULD SEE RIGHT THROUGH HIS WIFE; HE TOOK X-RAYS OF HER HAND	**$300**	WHO IS
NAMED FOR A PHYSICIAN BORN AROUND 460 B.C., IT INCLUDES A PLEDGE NOT TO SEDUCE A PATIENT'S SLAVES	**$400**	WHAT IS
THIS SYMBOL OF THE PHYSICIAN IS DERIVED FROM THE WAND OF AESCULAPIUS, THE GOD OF MEDICINE	**$500**	WHAT IS

JEOPARDY!

MEDICAL KNOWLEDGE

$100 WHAT IS DERMATOLOGY? **$100**

$200 WHAT IS A STETHOSCOPE? **$200**

$300 WHO IS WILHELM ROENTGEN? **$300**

$400 WHAT IS THE HIPPOCRATIC OATH? **$400**

$500 WHAT IS THE CADUCEUS? **$500**

JEOPARDY!

CHARLIE PARKER

Clue	Value	Response
PARKER WAS SELF-TAUGHT ON THIS MUSICAL INSTRUMENT HE GOT FROM HIS MOTHER AT AGE 11	**$100**	WHAT IS
FOREST WHITAKER PLAYED THE LEAD ROLE IN THIS DIRECTOR'S 1988 FILM "BIRD"	**$200**	WHO IS
DIZZY GILLESPIE, PARKER & OTHERS DEVELOPED THIS NEW STYLE OF JAZZ AT MINTON'S PLAYHOUSE, A NYC NIGHTCLUB	**$300**	WHAT IS
THIS MUSICAL BIRD "STUDY" BY PARKER WAS BASED ON THE CHORD PROGRESSIONS OF "HOW HIGH THE MOON"	**$400**	WHAT IS
DUE TO PARKER'S PROMINENCE, THIS LEADING NEW YORK CITY JAZZ CLUB WAS NAMED FOR HIM	**$500**	WHAT IS

JEOPARDY!

CHARLIE PARKER

$100 WHAT IS THE (ALTO) SAXOPHONE? **$100**

$200 WHO IS CLINT EASTWOOD? **$200**

$300 WHAT IS BEBOP? (ACCEPT: BOP) **$300**

$400 WHAT IS "ORNITHOLOGY"? **$400**

$500 WHAT IS BIRDLAND? **$500**

JEOPARDY!

"IN" & "OUT" PHRASES

A COOKING SITUATION THAT'S GONE FROM BAD TO WORSE	$100	WHAT IS
TO BE OUT OF FAVOR TEMPORARILY, AS WHEN MR. DARLING IN "PETER PAN" WAS EXILED TO NANA'S KENNEL	$200	WHAT IS
VISUAL CLICHE THAT'S THE OPPOSITE OF "ABSENCE MAKES THE HEART GROW FONDER"	$300	WHAT IS
LADY MACBETH'S 3-WORD LAMENT WHILE SLEEPWALKING, IT PRECEDES "OUT, I SAY!"	$400	WHAT IS
THIS LATIN PHRASE FROM HORACE MEANS "IN THE MIDST OF THINGS", ESPECIALLY OF A STORY	$500	WHAT IS

JEOPARDY!

"IN" & "OUT" PHRASES

$100	WHAT IS "OUT OF THE FRYING PAN AND INTO THE FIRE"?	**$100**
$200	WHAT IS "(TO BE) IN THE DOGHOUSE"?	**$200**
$300	WHAT IS "OUT OF SIGHT, OUT OF MIND"?	**$300**
$400	WHAT IS "OUT, DAMNED SPOT"?	**$400**
$500	WHAT IS "IN MEDIAS RES"?	**$500**

JEOPARDY!

WORK, WORK, WORK

Clue	Value	Response
SPECIFIC TERM FOR AN INVESTIGATOR OF INSURANCE CLAIMS	$100	WHAT IS
IN L.A. COUNTY JAILS, "INMATE WORKER" HAS REPLACED THIS TERM THAT'S A SYNONYM FOR "RELIABLE"	$200	WHAT IS
A CARNIVAL WORKER WHOM CUSTOMERS TRY TO DUNK, OR A LARRY HARMON CLOWN	$300	WHAT IS
TYPE OF "BANKER" WHO BUYS ISSUES OF STOCK & RESELLS THEM TO THE PUBLIC	$400	WHAT IS
BUSINESS OF THE LOIZEAUX FAMILY, KNOWN FOR THEIR WORK ON THE PRUITT-IGOE HOUSING PROJECT & THE SANDS HOTEL	$500	WHAT IS

JEOPARDY!

WORK, WORK, WORK

$100	WHAT IS AN ADJUSTER?	$100
$200	WHAT IS TRUSTY?	$200
$300	WHAT IS A BOZO?	$300
$400	WHAT IS AN INVESTMENT BANKER?	$400
$500	WHAT IS DEMOLITION?	$500

DOUBLE JEOPARDY!

LINES FROM LONGFELLOW

"FROM THE WATERFALL HE NAMED HER" THIS, MEANING "LAUGHING WATER"	**$200**	WHAT IS
DISTINGUISHING FEATURE OF THE GIRL WHO WAS VERY, VERY GOOD BUT "WHEN SHE WAS BAD SHE WAS HORRID"	**$400**	WHAT IS
THE 1874 BOOK OF "TALES FROM" HERE INCLUDES "PAUL REVERE'S RIDE" & THE LINE "SHIPS THAT PASS IN THE NIGHT"	**$600**	WHAT IS
THEY'RE WHAT WE CAN "LEAVE BEHIND US...ON THE SANDS OF TIME"	**$800**	WHAT ARE
"SANTA FILOMENA", ABOUT THIS WOMAN, STATES: "A LADY WITH A LAMP SHALL STAND IN THE GREAT HISTORY OF THE LAND"	**$1000**	WHO IS

DOUBLE JEOPARDY!

LINES FROM LONGFELLOW

$200   WHAT IS MINNEHAHA? $200

$400   WHAT IS A (LITTLE) CURL? $400

$600   WHAT IS "A WAYSIDE INN"? $600

$800   WHAT ARE FOOTPRINTS? $800

$1000   WHO IS FLORENCE NIGHTINGALE? $1000

DOUBLE JEOPARDY!

HISTORIC FIGURES

IN 1930 HE LED A MARCH TO THE SEA TO COLLECT SALT TO PROTEST A MONOPOLY BY THE GOVERNMENT OF INDIA	**$200**	WHO IS
IN 1979 THIS VICE-PREMIER BECAME THE FIRST TOP COMMUNIST LEADER FROM CHINA TO VISIT THE U.S.	**$400**	WHO IS
IN AN 1880 LETTER, QUEEN VICTORIA REFERRED TO THIS SUCCESSOR OF DISRAELI AS A "HALF-MAD FIRE-BRAND"	**$600**	WHO IS
THE EAGLE ON IRAQ'S COAT OF ARMS IS ASSOCIATED WITH THIS 12th CENTURY MUSLIM WARRIOR	**$800**	WHO IS
A LITTLE BIRDIE "PTOLD" ME: AFTER ALEXANDER THE GREAT'S DEATH, THIS GENERAL TOOK CONTROL OF EGYPT	**$1000**	WHO IS

DOUBLE JEOPARDY!

HISTORIC FIGURES

$200	WHO IS MOHANDAS (MAHATMA) GANDHI?	**$200**
$400	WHO IS DENG XIAOPING?	**$400**
$600	WHO IS WILLIAM GLADSTONE?	**$600**
$800	WHO IS SALADIN?	**$800**
$1000	WHO IS PTOLEMY(I)?	**$1000**

DOUBLE JEOPARDY!

POP MUSIC PEOPLE

THE SYMBOL THIS SINGER USED TO REPLACE HIS NAME WAS REFERRED TO AS A "GLYPH"	**$200**	WHO IS
SHE'S "THE QUEEN OF SOUL" &, ACCORDING TO THE KENNEDY CENTER HONORS, "AN ICON OF CONTEMPORARY POP MUSIC"	**$400**	WHO IS
THIS FORMER BOOMTOWN RATS LEADER WAS KNIGHTED FOR HIS FAMINE-RELIEF WORK	**$600**	WHO IS
THIS COUNTRY SUPERSTAR WAS BORN ON AUGUST 28, 1982	**$800**	WHO IS
WHEN HE & HIS WIFE JANE DIVORCED, WE DON'T KNOW IF SHE TOLD HIM, "DON'T COME AROUND HERE NO MORE"	**$1000**	WHO IS

DOUBLE JEOPARDY!

POP MUSIC PEOPLE

$200	WHO IS (THE ARTIST FORMERLY KNOWN AS) PRINCE?	$200
$400	WHO IS ARETHA FRANKLIN?	$400
$600	WHO IS (SIR) BOB GELDOF?	$600
$800	WHO IS LEANN RIMES?	$800
$1000	WHO IS TOM PETTY?	$1000

252

DOUBLE JEOPARDY!

INVESTMENT ADVICE

Clue	Value	Response
CONSIDER THE "WHOLE LIFE" TYPE OF THIS, UNLESS YOU'RE PLANNING TO DIE SOON	**$200**	WHAT IS
TO MINIMIZE YOUR RISK, BUY THESE "COLORFUL" STOCKS IN ESTABLISHED, RELIABLE COMPANIES	**$400**	WHAT ARE
DON'T BLOW YOUR MONEY ON RAP CDs (COMPACT DISCS), PUT IT IN ONE OF THESE BANK CDs	**$600**	WHAT IS
THIS NEW TYPE OF IRA NAMED FOR A SENATOR ALLOWS TAX-FREE WITHDRAWALS WHEN YOU'RE IN YOUR 60s	**$800**	WHAT IS
IF BUYING CORPORATE OR MUNICIPAL BONDS, YOU SHOULD KNOW THIS IS MOODY'S HIGHEST RATING	**$1000**	WHAT IS

DOUBLE JEOPARDY!

INVESTMENT ADVICE

$200 — WHAT IS (LIFE) INSURANCE? — $200

$400 — WHAT ARE BLUE CHIP (STOCKS)? — $400

$600 — WHAT IS A CERTIFICATE OF DEPOSIT? — $600

$800 — WHAT IS A ROTH IRA? — $800

$1000 — WHAT IS AAA? — $1000

DOUBLE JEOPARDY!

THE ANIMAL KINGDOM

Clue	Value	Response
YOU CAN'T CALL SNAKES SPINELESS: THEY MAY HAVE OVER 300 OF THESE BONES, COMPARED TO HUMANS' 33	**$200**	WHAT ARE
THIS TYPE OF CATFISH CAN GENERATE A 450-VOLT SHOCK, LESS THAN THE "EEL" OF THE SAME NAME	**$400**	WHAT IS
THE BARN SPECIES OF THIS BIRD IS SOMETIMES CALLED MONKEY-FACED DUE TO ITS SIMIAN FEATURES	**$600**	WHAT IS
AN ENDANGERED NORTH AFRICAN DEER IS CALLED THIS, LIKE AN "APE" FOUND ON GIBRALTAR	**$800**	WHAT IS
YOUNG RABBITS ARE BUNNIES; YOUNG ONES OF THESE ARE LEVERETS	**$1000**	WHAT ARE

DOUBLE JEOPARDY!

THE ANIMAL KINGDOM

$200	WHAT ARE VERTEBRAE? (ACCEPT: BACKBONES)	$200
$400	WHAT IS ELECTRIC?	$400
$600	WHAT IS THE OWL?	$600
$800	WHAT IS BARBARY (DEER OR STAG)?	$800
$1000	WHAT ARE HARES?	$1000

DOUBLE JEOPARDY!

GET "BACK"

SWIMMERS DO IT FACE UP WITH THEIR ARMS MOVING ALTERNATELY OVER THEIR HEADS	$200	WHAT IS
THIS GAME PLAYED ON A BOARD WITH 24 SPEAR-SHAPED POINTS MAY HAVE EVOLVED FROM PARCHEESI	$400	WHAT IS
USING THIS TECH-NIQUE, A PERSON CAN POSSIBLY CONTROL HIS OWN BLOOD PRESSURE & BODY TEMPERATURE	$600	WHAT IS
IT'S A VERY VOCAL SEA CREATURE WITH A CHARACTERISTIC ARCH OF THE BODY WHEN LEAPING	$800	WHAT IS
THEY'RE FAYETTEVILLE'S FAVORITE COLLEGE FOOTBALL TEAM	$1000	WHAT ARE

DOUBLE JEOPARDY!

GET "BACK"

$200	WHAT IS THE BACKSTROKE? (ACCEPT: BACKCRAWL)	**$200**
$400	WHAT IS BACKGAMMON?	**$400**
$600	WHAT IS BIOFEEDBACK?	**$600**
$800	WHAT IS A HUMPBACK WHALE?	**$800**
$1000	WHAT ARE THE (ARKANSAS) RAZORBACKS?	**$1000**

FINAL JEOPARDY!

POPULAR PSYCHOLOGY

THIS 1973 BOOK &
SUBSEQUENT TV MOVIE
POPULARIZED THE
STUDY OF MULTIPLE
PERSONALITY DISORDER

WHAT IS

FINAL JEOPARDY!

POPULAR PSYCHOLOGY

WHAT IS "SYBIL"?

JEOPARDY!

THE HIMALAYAS

IN SANSKRIT "HIMALAYA" MEANS "HOME OF" THIS SUBSTANCE	**$100**	WHAT IS
AN ICE CAVE AT OVER 10,000 FEET NEAR GANGOTRI IN THE HIMALAYAS IS THE SOURCE OF THIS SACRED INDIAN RIVER	**$200**	WHAT IS
THIS SHAGGY-HAIRED BEAST OF TIBET IS OFTEN CALLED THE GRUNTING OX BECAUSE OF THE SOUND IT MAKES	**$300**	WHAT IS
SOME HAVE SUGGESTED THAT THIS MYTHICAL HIMALAYAN CREATURE IS A PRE-HUMAN PRIMATE	**$400**	WHAT IS
THESE NEPALESE PEOPLE ARE MUCH SOUGHT AFTER AS PORTERS FOR HIMALAYAN CLIMBING EXPEDITIONS	**$500**	WHAT ARE

JEOPARDY!

THE HIMALAYAS

$100 | WHAT IS SNOW? | **$100**

$200 | WHAT IS THE GANGES RIVER? (ACCEPT: BHAGIRATHI) | **$200**

$300 | WHAT IS THE YAK? | **$300**

$400 | WHAT IS THE ABOMINABLE SNOWMAN? (ACCEPT: YETI) | **$400**

$500 | WHAT ARE THE SHERPAS? | **$500**

JEOPARDY!

GENERAL KNOWLEDGE

THE HOUSES OF LANCASTER & YORK USED DIFFERENT-COLORED TYPES OF THESE FLOWERS AS THEIR SYMBOLS	**$100**	WHAT ARE
NATIVE AMERICANS GREW THESE BEANS WITH CORN & AT HARVEST TIME COMBINED THEM INTO "M'SICKQUATASH"	**$200**	WHAT ARE
HE WAS THICK-SKULLED, HEAVY-BROWED, ABOUT 5 FEET TALL & NAMED FOR A PLACE IN GERMANY	**$300**	WHO IS
THE NUMBER OF DIFFERENT HEXAGRAMS IN THE I CHING, OR THE NUMBER OF SQUARES ON A CHECKERBOARD	**$400**	WHAT IS
2-WORD TERM FOR THE KEY WEEKDAY OF THE PRIMARY SEASON, LIKE MARCH 7, 2000	**$500**	WHAT IS

JEOPARDY!

GENERAL KNOWLEDGE

$100   WHAT ARE ROSES? $100

$200   WHAT ARE LIMA BEANS? $200

$300   WHO IS NEANDERTHAL MAN? $300

$400   WHAT IS 64? $400

$500   WHAT IS SUPER TUESDAY? $500

JEOPARDY!

WISCON-SIN

Clue	Value	Response
ON AUGUST 9, 1966 THE MILWAUKEE HQ OF THIS VENERABLE CIVIL RIGHTS ORGANIZATION WAS BOMBED	**$100**	WHAT IS
IN 1970 ACTIVISTS BLEW UP THE ARMY MATHEMATICS RESEARCH CENTER AT THE UNIVERSITY OF WISCONSIN IN THIS CITY	**$200**	WHAT IS
THIS CANNIBALISTIC SERIAL KILLER WAS SLAIN IN A WISCONSIN PRISON IN 1994	**$300**	WHO IS
IN A 1912 ASSASSI-NATION ATTEMPT, TEDDY ROOSEVELT WAS SAVED WHEN THE BULLET HIT THIS CASE IN HIS POCKET	**$400**	WHAT IS
A BOMB AT CAMPAIGN HQ IN MADISON DIDN'T STOP THE 1994 REELECTION OF TOMMY THOMPSON TO THIS OFFICE	**$500**	WHAT IS

JEOPARDY!™

WISCON-SIN

$100 — WHAT IS THE NAACP? — $100

$200 — WHAT IS MADISON? — $200

$300 — WHO IS JEFFREY DAHMER? — $300

$400 — WHAT IS HIS GLASSES CASE? — $400

$500 — WHAT IS GOVERNOR? — $500

JEOPARDY!

VOCALISTS

HE SANG "SONG SUNG BLUE" & "FOREVER IN BLUE JEANS"	**$100**	WHO IS
"YOU'RE SO VAIN" WAS A BESTSELLER FOR THIS PUBLISHING HEIRESS	**$200**	WHO IS
ONETIME COMMODORE WHO GAVE US "SAY YOU, SAY ME"	**$300**	WHO IS
HER LESS-THAN-TITANIC HITS INCLUDE "MISLED" & "NOTHING BROKEN BUT MY HEART"	**$400**	WHO IS
SHE SANG THE IMPASSIONED "I'M THE ONLY ONE" & "COME TO MY WINDOW"	**$500**	WHO IS

JEOPARDY!

VOCALISTS

$100 WHO IS NEIL DIAMOND? $100

$200 WHO IS CARLY SIMON? $200

$300 WHO IS LIONEL RICHIE? $300

$400 WHO IS CELINE DION? $400

$500 WHO IS MELISSA ETHERIDGE? $500

JEOPARDY!

THE MALE OF THE SPECIES

THIS BOY'S NAME IS GIVEN TO ANY MALE HOUSECAT	**$100**	WHAT IS
A HEN'S MATE, OR ANY BIRD THAT SETTLES ON A PERCH	**$200**	WHAT IS
THIS TERM FOR A MALE DUCK ALSO REFERS TO AN OLD TYPE OF CANNON	**$300**	WHAT IS
DOE, A RABBIT, A FEMALE RABBIT, & THIS, A MALE	**$400**	WHAT IS
WHEN MALE BADGERS & PIGS GET TOGETHER, THE FEMALES THINK THEY'RE A BUNCH OF THESE	**$500**	WHAT ARE

JEOPARDY!

THE MALE OF THE SPECIES

$100   WHAT IS A TOM (CAT)?   **$100**

$200   WHAT IS A ROOSTER?   **$200**

$300   WHAT IS A DRAKE?   **$300**

$400   WHAT IS A BUCK?   **$400**

$500   WHAT ARE BOARS?   **$500**

JEOPARDY!

VILIFICATION

ROSSINI SAID OF THIS "RING" LEADER, "HE HAS LOVELY MOMENTS BUT AWFUL QUARTERS OF AN HOUR"	**$100**	WHO IS
MARIO PUZO WROTE THAT ONE OF THESE MEN "WITH HIS BRIEF-CASE CAN STEAL MORE THAN A HUNDRED MEN WITH GUNS"	**$200**	WHAT IS
IN 1984 BARBARA BUSH SAID OF THIS VICE PRESIDENTIAL NOMINEE, "IT RHYMES WITH RICH", BUT LATER APOLOGIZED	**$300**	WHO IS
DOROTHY PARKER'S COMMENT ON THIS ACTRESS, "SHE RUNS THE GAMUT OF EMOTIONS FROM A TO B", WAS A JOKE	**$400**	WHO IS
HERMAN MANKIEWICZ SAID OF THIS DIRECTOR, "THERE, BUT FOR THE GRACE OF GOD, GOES GOD"	**$500**	WHO IS

JEOPARDY!

VILIFICATION

$100   WHO IS
RICHARD WAGNER? $100

$200   WHAT IS A LAWYER? $200

$300   WHO IS
GERALDINE FERRARO? $300

$400   WHO IS
KATHARINE HEPBURN? $400

$500   WHO IS
ORSON WELLES? $500

DOUBLE JEOPARDY!

CONFEDERATES

THIS AUTHOR & STEAMBOAT PILOT'S CIVIL WAR EXPERIENCE WAS SERVING ABOUT A MONTH IN THE MISSOURI MILITIA	**$200**	WHO IS
THIS NICKNAME THAT GENERAL BARNARD BEE GAVE THOMAS JACKSON MAY HAVE BEEN AN INSULT	**$400**	WHAT IS
PIERRE G.T. BEAUREGARD WAS KNOWN AS "THE LITTLE" THIS FROM HIS ADMIRATION OF THE FRENCH LEADER	**$600**	WHAT IS
GENERAL JOSEPH JOHNSTON'S ARRIVAL HELPED THE SOUTH WIN THE JULY 1861 FIRST BATTLE OF THIS VIRGINIA PLACE	**$800**	WHAT IS
HE NEVER FORGAVE LEE FOR HAVING HIM SEND HIS MEN ON THAT DOOMED CHARGE AT GETTYSBURG	**$1000**	WHO IS

DOUBLE JEOPARDY!

CONFEDERATES

$200	WHO IS MARK TWAIN? (ACCEPT: SAMUEL CLEMENS)	$200
$400	WHAT IS STONEWALL?	$400
$600	WHAT IS NAPOLEON?	$600
$800	WHAT IS BULL RUN? (ACCEPT: MANASSAS)	$800
$1000	WHO IS GEORGE EDWARD PICKETT?	$1000

DOUBLE JEOPARDY!

MEDICAL MEN

IN THE 1980s ROBERT GALLO IDENTIFIED THIS AIDS-CAUSING VIRUS BUT CALLED IT HTLV	**$200**	WHAT IS
THIS NOVELIST & MEDICAL SCHOOL GRADUATE (HARVARD '69) CREATED THE TV SHOW "ER"	**$400**	WHO IS
STANLEY PRUSINER'S THEORY OF PRIONS MAY EXPLAIN THIS DISEASE ALSO CALLED BOVINE SPONGIFORM ENCEPHALOPATHY	**$600**	WHAT IS
A TYPE OF CHOREA, A NERVE DISEASE, IS NAMED FOR THIS PHYSICIAN WHO DIED IN 1916	**$800**	WHO IS
THIS ENGLISH DIS-COVERER OF BLOOD CIRCULATION STUDIED AT PADUA WITH THE GREAT ANATOMIST AQUAPENDENTE	**$1000**	WHO IS

DOUBLE JEOPARDY!

MEDICAL MEN

$200   WHAT IS HIV? $200

$400   WHO IS MICHAEL CRICHTON? $400

$600   WHAT IS MAD COW DISEASE? $600

$800   WHO IS GEORGE S. HUNTINGTON? $800

$1000   WHO IS WILLIAM HARVEY? $1000

DOUBLE JEOPARDY!

THE "BIG" SCREEN

IN IT, PAUL REUBENS' ALTER EGO JOINS THE CIRCUS	**$200**	WHAT IS
IT'S THE 1970 DUSTIN HOFFMAN FILM WITH THE LINE "IT'S A GOOD DAY TO DIE"	**$400**	WHAT IS
HUMPHREY BOGART PLAYED PHILIP MARLOWE IN THIS 1946 FILM	**$600**	WHAT IS
LEE MARVIN & MARK HAMILL STARRED IN THIS 1980 SAM FULLER FILM FULL OF WWII STORIES	**$800**	WHAT IS
THIS COEN BROTHERS FILM STARRING JEFF BRIDGES FEATURED JOHN TURTURRO AS AN EGOMANIACAL BOWLER	**$1000**	WHAT IS

DOUBLE JEOPARDY!

THE "BIG" SCREEN

$200   WHAT IS "BIG TOP PEE WEE"? $200

$400   WHAT IS "LITTLE BIG MAN"? $400

$600   WHAT IS "THE BIG SLEEP"? $600

$800   WHAT IS "THE BIG RED ONE"? $800

$1000   WHAT IS "THE BIG LEBOWSKI"? $1000

DOUBLE JEOPARDY!

STREET SMARTS

IT'S SYNONYMOUS WITH THE STOCK MARKET	**$200**	WHAT IS
WHILE BRITISH PRIME MINISTER, MARGARET THATCHER HAD GATES PUT UP ON THE WHITEHALL END OF THIS STREET	**$400**	WHAT IS
WE WONDER IF GENERAL GRANT WAS SINGING THE BLUES WHEN HE SET UP HEADQUARTERS ON THIS MEMPHIS STREET	**$600**	WHAT IS
STREETS IN THIS CITY INCLUDE RALPH DAVID ABERNATHY BOULEVARD & COCA COLA PLACE	**$800**	WHAT IS
SAN FRANCISCO THROUGHFARE KNOWN AS "THE CROOKEDEST STREET IN THE WORLD"	**$1000**	WHAT IS

DOUBLE JEOPARDY!

STREET SMARTS

$200	WHAT IS WALL STREET?	**$200**
$400	WHAT IS DOWNING STREET?	**$400**
$600	WHAT IS BEALE STREET?	**$600**
$800	WHAT IS ATLANTA?	**$800**
$1000	WHAT IS LOMBARD STREET?	**$1000**

DOUBLE JEOPARDY!

LAZYBONES

Clue	Value	Response
TRADEMARK NAME OF A SHOE INDICATING IT'S MEANT FOR THOSE TOO LAZY TO LACE & TIE	**$200**	WHAT IS
IN AN AESOP FABLE, THESE INSECTS LAUGH AT A HUNGRY CICADA WHO GOOFED OFF ALL SUMMER	**$400**	WHAT ARE
PROVERBIALLY, "THE DEVIL FINDS WORK FOR" THESE "TO DO"	**$600**	WHAT ARE
IT'S RICHARD LINK-LATER'S 1991 FILM ABOUT THE SUB-CULTURE OF AUSTIN, TEXAS DROPOUTS & HANGERS-OUT	**$800**	WHAT IS
IN THE 1948 CAMPAIGN, IT WAS TRUMAN'S FAVORITE ADJECTIVE FOR THE REPUBLICAN 80th CONGRESS	**$1000**	WHAT IS

DOUBLE JEOPARDY!

LAZYBONES

$200	WHAT IS (A) LOAFER?	**$200**
$400	WHAT ARE ANTS?	**$400**
$600	WHAT ARE IDLE HANDS?	**$600**
$800	WHAT IS "SLACKER"?	**$800**
$1000	WHAT IS DO-NOTHING?	**$1000**

DOUBLE JEOPARDY!

FICTIONAL FOLKS

HUCK, AS IN HUCK FINN, IS SHORT FOR THIS	**$200**	WHAT IS
HE GAVE CHARLIE A TOUR OF HIS CHOCOLATE FACTORY	**$400**	WHO IS
1938 DAPHNE DU MAURIER NOVEL IN WHICH YOU FIND THE SECOND MRS. DE WINTER OF OUR DISCONTENT	**$600**	WHAT IS
THIS AUTHOR FELT HE HAD NO CHOICE BUT TO CREATE SOPHIE ZAWISTOWSKA	**$800**	WHO IS
A SINCLAIR LEWIS NOVEL ENDS WITH THIS PREACHER'S LINE "WE SHALL YET MAKE THESE UNITED STATES A MORAL NATION!"	**$1000**	WHO IS

DOUBLE JEOPARDY!

FICTIONAL FOLKS

$200	WHAT IS HUCKLEBERRY?	$200
$400	WHO IS WILLY WONKA?	$400
$600	WHAT IS "REBECCA"?	$600
$800	WHO IS WILLIAM STYRON?	$800
$1000	WHO IS ELMER GANTRY?	$1000

FINAL JEOPARDY!

THE COLD WAR

28 YEARS APART, THEY
ARE THE YEAR THE BERLIN
WALL ERECTED & THE YEAR
IT WAS TORN DOWN

WHAT ARE

FINAL JEOPARDY!

THE COLD WAR

WHAT ARE 1961 & 1989?

JEOPARDY!

HAIL TO THE CHIEF

IN 1974, AS GOVERNOR OF GEORGIA, HE APPEARED ON "WHAT'S MY LINE?" & STUMPED THE PANEL	**$100**	WHO IS
ISSUED IN 1862, A 10-DOLLAR NOTE DEPICTING HIM WAS THE FIRST U.S. CURRENCY TO FEATURE A LIVING PRESIDENT	**$200**	WHO IS
HE WAS BORN JAN. 30, 1882, IN HYDE PARK, NEW YORK	**$300**	WHO IS
HE WAS HAPPIER BEING CHIEF JUSTICE THAN PRESIDENT, & PROBABLY HAPPIER STILL WITH A BIG SLICE OF PIE IN FRONT OF HIM	**$400**	WHO IS
HE CLAIMED THE SMEAR & SLANDER TACTICS OF THE 1828 ELECTION DROVE HIS WIFE RACHEL TO HER GRAVE	**$500**	WHO IS

JEOPARDY!

HAIL TO THE CHIEF

$100   WHO IS JIMMY CARTER? $100

$200   WHO IS ABRAHAM LINCOLN? $200

$300   WHO IS FRANKLIN D. ROOSEVELT? $300

$400   WHO IS WILLIAM HOWARD TAFT? $400

$500   WHO IS ANDREW JACKSON? $500

JEOPARDY!

BRIT LIT

SHE HAD HER LOVER & FUTURE HUSBAND PERCY EDIT HER FIRST NOVEL, "FRANKENSTEIN"	**$100**	WHO IS
HIS OWN DISASTROUS TRIP TO THE CONGO IN 1890 WAS THE BASIS FOR HIS "HEART OF DARKNESS"	**$200**	WHO IS
HE WROTE ABOUT GUNGA DASS AS WELL AS GUNGA DIN	**$300**	WHO IS
IN 1816 SHE REVISED HER "NORTHANGER ABBEY"; SHE ORIGINALLY PLANNED TO PUBLISH IT IN 1803	**$400**	WHO IS
IN 1914's "THE WORLD SET FREE", HE WROTE OF A WAR IN 1958 INVOLVING ATOMIC BOMBS	**$500**	WHO IS

JEOPARDY!

BRIT LIT

$100	WHO IS MARY (WOLLSTONECRAFT) SHELLEY?	**$100**
$200	WHO IS JOSEPH CONRAD?	**$200**
$300	WHO IS (JOSEPH) RUDYARD KIPLING?	**$300**
$400	WHO IS JANE AUSTEN?	**$400**
$500	WHO IS H.G. WELLS? (ACCEPT: HERBERT GEORGE WELLS)	**$500**

JEOPARDY!

SEAFOOD DIET

THE SOCKEYE SPECIES OF THIS FISH IS HIGHLY PRIZED FOR CANNING	**$100**	WHAT IS
PROBABLY THE FIRST FISH RAISED IN CAPTIVITY, THE RAINBOW SPECIES OF THIS FISH IS MOST COMMONLY FOUND ON FARMS	**$200**	WHAT IS
CALAMARI, ANOTHER NAME FOR THIS MOLLUSK WITH AN EDIBLE INK, COMES FROM THE LATIN FOR "WRITING PEN"	**$300**	WHAT IS
TOP QUALITY CAVIAR CONTAINS LESS THAN 5% OF THIS ADDITIVE	**$400**	WHAT IS
A METALWORKER WOULD KNOW THE NAME OF THIS SMALL, SILVERY FISH USUALLY FRIED & EATEN WHOLE	**$500**	WHAT IS

JEOPARDY!

SEAFOOD DIET

$100   WHAT IS THE SALMON? $100

$200   WHAT IS THE TROUT? $200

$300   WHAT IS THE SQUID? $300

$400   WHAT IS SALT? $400

$500   WHAT IS THE SMELT? $500

JEOPARDY!

ANAGRAMMED COUNTRIES

TANGO	**$100**	WHAT IS
LIZ BRA	**$200**	WHAT IS
PAL DON	**$300**	WHAT IS
GOON MAIL	**$400**	WHAT IS
SAND HOUR	**$500**	WHAT IS

JEOPARDY!

ANAGRAMMED COUNTRIES

$100	WHAT IS TONGA?	**$100**
$200	WHAT IS BRAZIL?	**$200**
$300	WHAT IS POLAND?	**$300**
$400	WHAT IS MONGOLIA?	**$400**
$500	WHAT IS HONDURAS?	**$500**

JEOPARDY!

ACTORS IN HITCHCOCK FILMS

A GOOD GUY AS PERRY MASON, HE PLAYED THE BAD GUY JIMMY STEWART SPIED ON IN "REAR WINDOW"	**$100**	WHO IS
BEFORE HE PLAYED TED BAXTER, TED KNIGHT HAD A BIT ROLE AS A COP GUARDING NORMAN BATES IN THIS 1960 FILM	**$200**	WHAT IS
SUZANNE PLESHETTE IS FOUND PECKED TO DEATH IN THIS 1963 CLASSIC	**$300**	WHAT IS
FILM IN WHICH ROBERT WALKER PROPOSES A BLOODY BARGAIN TO FARLEY GRANGER WHILE TRAVELING	**$400**	WHAT IS
DIANE LADD KNOWS THIS ACTOR, HER EX-HUSBAND, APPEARED AS A SAILOR IN "MARNIE"	**$500**	WHO IS

JEOPARDY!

ACTORS IN HITCHCOCK FILMS

$100	WHO IS RAYMOND BURR?	**$100**
$200	WHAT IS "PSYCHO"?	**$200**
$300	WHAT IS "THE BIRDS"?	**$300**
$400	WHAT IS "STRANGERS ON A TRAIN"?	**$400**
$500	WHO IS BRUCE DERN?	**$500**

JEOPARDY!

SKIN DEEP

Clue	Value	Response
WRINKLES AT THE CORNER OF THE EYE, PERHAPS CAUSED BY SQUINTING WHILE BIRDWATCHING	**$100**	WHAT ARE
THE COASTERS MIGHT KNOW CONTACT DERMATITIS CAN BE THE RESULT OF CONTACT WITH THIS PLANT	**$200**	WHAT IS
THE LITTLE SECTIONS OF DEAD EPIDERMIS AROUND YOUR FINGERNAILS	**$300**	WHAT ARE
THIS TERM FOR A BALM FOR THE SKIN OR THE CONSCIENCE GOES BACK TO THE SANSKRIT SARPIS, "MELTED BUTTER"	**$400**	WHAT IS
THE SKIN'S 2 EXOCRINE TYPES OF GLANDS ARE SWEAT GLANDS & THESE, WHICH PRODUCE OILS	**$500**	WHAT ARE

JEOPARDY!

SKIN DEEP

$100	WHAT ARE CROW'S FEET?	$100
$200	WHAT IS POISON IVY?	$200
$300	WHAT ARE CUTICLES?	$300
$400	WHAT IS SALVE?	$400
$500	WHAT ARE SEBACEOUS GLANDS?	$500

DOUBLE JEOPARDY!

BROOKLYN NEIGHBORHOODS

IN 1968 THIS AREA CALLED "BED-STUY" ELECTED SHIRLEY CHISHOLM, THE FIRST BLACK WOMAN IN CONGRESS	**$200**	WHAT IS
CREATED IN 1903, LUNA PARK IN THIS AMUSEMENT AREA WAS SORT OF AN EARLY VERSION OF FANTASYLAND	**$400**	WHAT IS
A STREET GANG IN A 1974 FILM WAS CALLED "THE LORDS OF" THIS LARGE BROOKLYN NEIGHBORHOOD	**$600**	WHAT IS
AS THE SETTING FOR "THE HONEY-MOONERS", THIS AREA IN SW BROOKLYN COULD BE CALLED KRAMDENHURST	**$800**	WHAT IS
THESE "HEIGHTS" POPULATED BY AFRICAN-AMERICANS & HASIDIC JEWS WERE THE SITE OF RIOTING IN 1991	**$1000**	WHAT IS

DOUBLE JEOPARDY!

BROOKLYN NEIGHBORHOODS

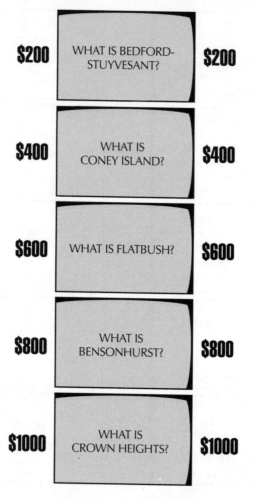

$200	WHAT IS BEDFORD-STUYVESANT?	$200
$400	WHAT IS CONEY ISLAND?	$400
$600	WHAT IS FLATBUSH?	$600
$800	WHAT IS BENSONHURST?	$800
$1000	WHAT IS CROWN HEIGHTS?	$1000

DOUBLE JEOPARDY!

TALES TO TELL

IN 1851 HE PUBLISHED LITERATURE'S BEST-KNOWN WHALE TALE	**$200**	WHO IS
ARTHUR C. CLARKE FOLLOWED HIS BOOK "THE NINE BILLION NAMES OF GOD" WITH THIS OTHER NUMERI-CALLY TITLED TALE	**$400**	WHAT IS
BE THANKFUL WE'RE NOT GOING TO LIST ALL THE CHARACTERS IN HIS "GRAVITY'S RAINBOW"; THERE ARE OVER 400	**$600**	WHO IS
THIS 1993 ROBERT ALTMAN FILM WAS BASED ON A FEW TALES OF RAYMOND CARVER	**$800**	WHAT IS
THE UPSHOT IS HE WON THE HOWELLS MEDAL FOR HIS "WAPSHOT SCANDAL"	**$1000**	WHO IS

DOUBLE JEOPARDY!

TALES TO TELL

$200	WHO IS HERMAN MELVILLE?
$400	WHAT IS "2001: (A SPACE ODYSSEY)"?
$600	WHO IS THOMAS PYNCHON?
$800	WHAT IS "SHORT CUTS"?
$1000	WHO IS JOHN CHEEVER?

DOUBLE JEOPARDY!

... "UM"

IT HOLDS TWICE AS MUCH AS THE USUAL WINE OR CHAMPAGNE BOTTLE	**$200**	WHAT IS
IT'S A FINAL DEMAND OR STATEMENT OF CONDITIONS; DON'T MAKE ME GIVE YOU ONE	**$400**	WHAT IS
IT'S THE CLEAR, THIN PART OF THE BLOOD THAT REMAINS AFTER CLOTTING	**$600**	WHAT IS
HYDROGEN IS THE ONLY CHEMICAL ELEMENT THAT'S LIGHTER THAN THIS ONE	**$800**	WHAT IS
HE ALSO SCULPTED THE HEAD OF ABRAHAM LINCOLN FOR THE CAPITOL ROTUNDA	**$1000**	WHO IS

DOUBLE JEOPARDY!

... "UM"

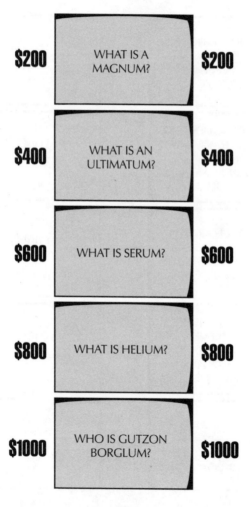

$200   WHAT IS A MAGNUM? $200

$400   WHAT IS AN ULTIMATUM? $400

$600   WHAT IS SERUM? $600

$800   WHAT IS HELIUM? $800

$1000   WHO IS GUTZON BORGLUM? $1000

DOUBLE JEOPARDY!

THE POLICE

Clue	Value	Response
SIR ROBERT PEEL ORGANIZED THIS CITY'S POLICE FORCE IN 1829 & THEY'VE BEEN NICKNAMED FOR HIM EVER SINCE	$200	WHAT IS
THIS WORD FOR A FRENCH POLICEMAN COMES FROM AN OLDER WORD MEANING PEOPLE-AT-ARMS	$400	WHAT IS
THEY WERE ONCE CALLED THE NORTH-WEST MOUNTED POLICE; NOW THEY PROTECT THE NORTH-WEST TERRITORIES	$600	WHAT IS
THIS COUNTRY'S CARABINIERI EVOLVED FROM A MILITARY GROUP THAT SERVED THE SAVOYARD STATES	$800	WHAT IS
THE NATIONAL POLICE FORCES OF ABOUT 180 COUNTRIES ARE MEMBERS OF THIS COOPERATIVE ORGANIZATION	$1000	WHAT IS

DOUBLE JEOPARDY!

THE POLICE

$200   WHAT IS LONDON? $200

$400   WHAT IS A GENDARME? $400

$600   WHAT IS THE ROYAL CANADIAN MOUNTED POLICE? $600

$800   WHAT IS ITALY? $800

$1000   WHAT IS INTERPOL? $1000

DOUBLE JEOPARDY!

LOOK!

Clue	Value	Response
OPERATION LIFESAVER ENCOURAGES DRIVERS TO "LOOK, LISTEN AND LIVE!" WHEN CROSSING THESE	$200	WHAT ARE
IF YOU HEAR THIS SHOUT ON A GOLF COURSE, LOOK UP FOR INCOMING GOLF BALLS	$400	WHAT IS
IT MEANS TO TAKE A QUICK LOOK, OR TO HIT SOMETHING AT AN ANGLE & BOUNCE OFF	$600	WHAT IS
IF YOU'RE STARING AT SOMEONE, YOU MAY BE ADVISED TO DO THIS— "IT'LL LAST LONGER"	$800	WHAT IS
LOOKOUT MOUNTAIN JUST SOUTH OF THIS SOUTHERN TENNESSEE CITY OFFERS TOURISTS A VIEW OF 7 STATES	$1000	WHAT IS

DOUBLE JEOPARDY!

LOOK!

$200	WHAT ARE RAILROAD TRACKS?	**$200**
$400	WHAT IS FORE!?	**$400**
$600	WHAT IS TO GLANCE?	**$600**
$800	WHAT IS TAKE A PICTURE?	**$800**
$1000	WHAT IS CHATTANOOGA?	**$1000**

DOUBLE JEOPARDY!

OFF THE AIR

THIS SITCOM WAS WELL INTO ITS FIRST SEASON WHEN JALEEL WHITE JOINED IT AS STEVE URKEL	**$200**	WHAT IS
FRIENDS OF THIS JAMES GARNER CHARACTER INCLUDED LAWYER BETH, POLICE DETECTIVE DENNIS & A PONTIAC FIREBIRD	**$400**	WHO IS
BOB NEWHART & THIS "TAXI" STAR TEAMED UP FOR "GEORGE & LEO", DESCRIBED AS "MORE GRUMPIER OLD MEN"	**$600**	WHO IS
IN THE EARLY '60s MARTIN MILNER & GEORGE MAHARIS GOT THEIR KICKS ON THIS SERIES	**$800**	WHAT IS
STARTING IN 1974 BERT CONVY HOSTED THIS GAME SHOW THAT FEATURED CELEBRITY COUPLES	**$1000**	WHAT IS

DOUBLE JEOPARDY!

OFF THE AIR

$200 | WHAT IS "FAMILY MATTERS"? | $200

$400 | WHO IS JIM ROCKFORD? | $400

$600 | WHO IS JUDD HIRSCH? | $600

$800 | WHAT IS "ROUTE 66"? | $800

$1000 | WHAT IS "TATTLETALES"? | $1000

FINAL JEOPARDY!
20th CENTURY NAMES

IN 1916, HIS VERY
PERSISTENT ASSASSINS
INCLUDED A PRINCE
& A GRAND DUKE

WHO IS

FINAL JEOPARDY!
20th CENTURY NAMES

WHO IS RASPUTIN?